Social Organization in Aboriginal Australia

Warren Shapiro

St. Martin's Press
New York
1979

All rights reserved. For information, write:
St. Martin's Press, Inc., 175 Fifth Avenue, New York, N.Y. 10010
Printed in Australia
First published in the United States of America in 1979
ISBN 0-312-73316-X

Library of Congress Cataloging in Publication Data
Shapiro, Warren.
   Social organization in aboriginal Australia.
   Bibliography: p.
   Includes index.
   1. Australian aborigines. 2. Ethnology—Australia.
I. Title.
GN665.S52 1979   301.4'00994   78-32074
ISBN 0-312-73316-X

To Emeritus Professor A. P. Elkin

Preface

This book is directed primarily at that famous literary figure, the 'generally educated reader', who may find some of it a bit rough going. I should like to think such difficulties would derive inevitably from the nature of the subject-matter, rather than from my own limitations; but I confess to some uncertainty. I should also be less than candid if I were to pretend that there is no wish on my part to say something here to my professional colleagues.

Work on this book began in 1973. In 1974 the American edition appeared of Kenneth Maddock's *The Australian Aborigines: a portrait of their society*, to which the present effort is plainly rival. I have not thought it necessary to revise my manuscript to take account of Maddock's book, in part because much of it is foreshadowed in his earlier articles (see References). More important, I consider *The Australian Aborigines* to be an extraordinary example of how Aboriginal ethnography can be misrepresented, so as to jibe with Lévi-Strauss (1969a); and I deal with the latter in some detail in chapter 10. A critique of Maddock would thus be largely redundant.

In 1975 I returned to Australia to carry out ethnographic research with some of the more southerly Aboriginal peoples of Arnhem Land: these adjoin and are related to the north-east Arnhem Landers, with whom I worked in 1965-67. My 1975 research enabled me to put north-east Arnhem Land social classification in broader perspective, and it caused me to doubt at least one of my earlier conclusions: the equifocality of *mukul bapa* and *mukul rumaru* in Arnhem Land kin-classification (pp. 6). Earlier this year, Professor H. W. Scheffler was kind enough to allow me to read the manuscript of his forthcoming comparative study of Aboriginal relationship terminologies; and this crystallized my doubt. I now believe that *mukul bapa* is the focal subcategory of the *mukul* category, from which *mukul rumaru* is derived. I have not, however, altered this book to incorporate this new conclusion—mainly because equifocality in this domain is important enough to warrant an illustration, even a mistaken one.

I have to thank Professor Scheffler, and Professor Ward Goodenough, for their profound influence on my thinking on matters pertinent to this book, and more expressly, for critically reading it in manuscript. Thanks are also due to the Research School of Pacific Studies of The Australian National University for supporting my 1965-67 research; and the American Philosophical Society, the Australian Institute of Aboriginal Studies, and the Rutgers University Research Council for footing my 1975 bills. All quotations from A. P. Elkin's *The Australian Aborigines* are used by permission of Messrs Angus & Robertson, Sydney. I wish, finally, to express my gratitude to the staff of The Australian National University Press, for putting up with my querying and emendatory letters from halfway around the globe.

New York City
July 1977   W.S.

Contents

Map

Introduction

The influence of Aboriginal Australia on the social sciences is by no means confined to that esoteric branch of anthropology known as 'kinship studies'. Still, from its beginning, major practitioners of this mini-discipline have looked to the first Australians for illustration and resolution of their theories. Lewis Henry Morgan, generally acknowledged as the pioneer of modern kinship studies, believed that the domestic life and kin-classifications of the Aborigines represent an early stage in human social evolution, a stage through which Western societies had long ago passed (Morgan, 1877). Early in the present century Morgan's scheme was demolished in the United States by Robert Lowie, who also appealed to Australian data (Lowie, 1920, pp. 147-85), and in Great Britain by the Anglicized Pole Bronislaw Malinowski, who devoted an entire volume (Malinowski, 1913) to a critical review of what was then known about Aboriginal domestic and marital institutions. Another notable British anthropologist of the day, A. R. Radcliffe-Brown, built his reputation as a theorist through comparative study of Aboriginal social organizations. His major work in this field (Radcliffe-Brown, 1931) is even today considered by many (myself not among them) as definitive.

This influence has been felt across the Channel too. Radcliffe-Brown was inspired by the Frenchman Emile Durkheim, who combined Morgan's preoccupation with the evolution of social forms with a more cognitive orientation (Durkheim, 1915; Durkheim and Mauss, 1963, 1st ed. 1903). More contemporary in this tradition is Durkheim's countryman, the celebrated Claude Lévi-Strauss, who has written no fewer than

1

three books which have largely to do with Aboriginal social organization (Lévi-Strauss, 1962, 1966, 1969a). Lévi-Strauss has numerous disciples, both within and outside the borders of France, of whom Robin Fox, Louis Dumont, and Edmund Leach need to be singled out here. Fox has taken the Master's more behavioural approaches to Aboriginal marriage and incorporated them into an introductory text (Fox, 1967a); Dumont has grasped the later, more cognitively-oriented Lévi-Strauss, and from this base has proceeded to re-examine certain marital institutions in both India and Australia (Dumont, 1957, 1966); and Leach has alternatively embraced both Lévi-Straussian styles (compare, for example, Leach, 1961c, chs. 3 and 6).

I shall return to these anthropologists later. But now the question: Why have they, and so many others, paid so much attention to the Aboriginal data? Which is to say, what is it about Aboriginal social organization and socioeconomic life generally that has attracted major social theorists since the middle of the last century?

First, when they were discovered by 'Europeans', Aborigines everywhere lived by hunting wild animals and foraging for wild plants—just as our own ancestors did until about ten thousand years ago, when someone somewhere in the Middle East began to 'domesticate' certain varieties of the local wildlife. Aborigines, however, knew nothing of farming and raising animals for meat, milk, and transport—the technological vertebrae of what we are pleased to call our urban civilization (Smith, 1972).

Second, unlike most peoples who subsist by foraging, Aborigines developed their cultures for milennia in relative isolation from technologically more advanced societies. Australia was peopled for perhaps as long as 40,000 years before the coming of Europeans at the end of the eighteenth century, and during this long period almost all exercises in 'international relations' were between one foraging group and another.[1] Now this is no small

---

[1] Gould (1973) provides a handy introduction to Australian archaeology as well as an extensive bibliography on the subject. For information on contact with non-Aborigines, see Macknight (1972) and the bibliography therein, and the collections of essays edited by Pilling and Waterman (1970) and Reay (1964).

consideration, for we are beginning to realize that foragers who live in a world of foragers are quite different from those who do not (Gardner, 1966). Our ancestors, remember, were of the first stripe; hence we are probably better justified in seeking their like in Aboriginal Australia than among, say, the South African Bushmen. This is not to argue that Morgan was right—only that he knew where to look.

Third, as is the case with most foraging peoples, Aboriginal societies in the main lack economic and political specializations which are independent of more elementary criteria of social organization, such as age, sex, and personal attributes. Thus any man who is not too old is a hunter, any woman who is not too old a forager. These societies are sometimes said to lack 'government', which is true in that they have nothing comparable to kings, cabinets, or congresses, presidents, prime ministers, or parliaments. But very considerable power is exercised by elder males, especially in pursuit of their individual interests but also collectively (Meggitt, 1964; Rose, 1968).

Last but certainly not least, Aboriginal social organizations have been described as 'complex'—all the more remarkably so because of the 'simplicity' of the associated technologies. This is misleading: anthropologists who subscribe to this notion are only advertising their inability to grasp what every Aboriginal knows from adolescence onwards. In fact, these social organizations are founded upon the six criteria that underlie human society everywhere: age, sex, kinship and affinity, locality, comradeship, and personal attributes. It is true that they have pushed some of these—most notably kinship and affinity—rather far, but this is 'elaboration', not 'complexity'. The social distinctions that complicate our lives—town/country, haves/have-nots, management/labour, etc.—are either totally absent from Aboriginal Australia, or exist as rudimentary derivatives of one or more of the six more general principles.

Of these six, age and sex are relatively obvious and will not get detailed treatment here. Aboriginal use of personal anatomical and behavioural traits to generate social categories—e.g. 'lefty', 'shorty', 'loner'—will be treated only lightly too, though it dovetails, as Lévi-Strauss (1966) has shown, with other principles of social classification. The same goes for comradeship: Aborigines, like other human beings, make friends, but my sole concern here is with the other social criteria that make friendship possible.

My focus will be on kinship and affinity, because this is what Aborigines are most famous for, and because, in my view, there is no satisfactory explication of this subject yet in print. So I ought to examine a couple of terms. Kinship, a familiar word in more ways than one, can thus stand as is, at least for a while. Affinity means 'relationship through marriage': my wife is an *affinal* relative or *affine*, as is my father-in-law, mother-in-law, brother-in-law, etc. We cannot assume, however, that in every culture the same set of relatives is classed as 'affinal'; and we may not even be entirely safe in assuming that 'affinity' is a meaningful term in the analysis of all cultures (Adams, 1960; cf. Goodenough, 1970, pp. 19-21). Still less should we think that our separation of 'blood-kin'—the anthropologist's technical terms are *consanguine* and *cognate*—from affines is everywhere applicable. And finally, the cross-cultural utility of such a simple term as 'marriage' has been critically scrutinized by anthropologists. All this is by way of an alert, for we will come upon most of these issues again.

I have so far considered five of the six elementary principles of social classification; but I have said nothing about locality. This is not because it is not linked to kinship and affinity in Aboriginal Australia—it is; or because it is of little significance—it is of the utmost importance in grasping the conceptual world of the first Australians. Which accounts for my reticence. Let me explain.

The origins of Aboriginal culture are elucidated by a set of stories, which also accounts for many natural features, including those of the lands occupied by the people themselves. These stories are the property of certain groups. They are told to males of the appropriate groups at around puberty and to other males later, if these have earned the goodwill of the owners. But they are not communicated lightly. Men who hear them are heavily indebted to the owners, usurpation of ownership is punishable by death, and, at least in theory, they cannot be told to females.

Many Europeans, including some anthropologists, who have dealt with Aborigines, have not taken these considerations very seriously. It is doubtless appropriate to communicate these sacred stories and to make photographs or films of corresponding rituals available to colleagues and other serious students of Aboriginal life. This is, I think, in keeping with the respect enjoined by the Aborigines towards these things, and it is surely a professional obligation. As for the exclusion of females, this is clearly against the currents of our own time and place; and there are indications that the Aborigines themselves are beginning to emancipate their women (Berndt, 1962).

But the revelation of these sacred materials to novices—male or female—is quite another matter. I see no justification for it, yet it has been done in scores of popular books and periodicals. Since this book is directed toward those who have no previous knowledge of Aboriginal Australians, I must assume that its readers are not yet ready for what that great authority A. P. Elkin has called 'the secret life of the Australian Aborigines'. I shall accordingly, when considering Aboriginal local organization, say very little about the associated myths and rituals, and I shall supply no references to sacred materials in these contexts. Should you decide to seek out this knowledge independently, I shall content myself with the probability that this shows sufficient interest and respect to enable you properly to have it.

My own direct knowledge of Aborigines stems from sixteen months in the north-eastern part of the Arnhem Land reserve in 1965-67 (Map 1). Otherwise I have read, I think, most of what has been written on Aboriginal social organization, both ethnographic ('descriptive') and theoretical, and I have talked with many individuals who have had similar experiences. All this has led me to believe that there really is *an* Aboriginal social organization, a set of themes which, in an area of nearly three million square miles, can naturally be expected to have several variations. I shall often call attention to these variations because of their importance in anthropological theory, or else to add vividness to more general considerations; but my dominant approach will be a 'least common denominator' one. Sometimes my conclusions will be based upon inadequate information, in which cases I shall say so. Elsewhere I shall take one side in an anthropological debate, but then I shall give my reasons for rejecting the other side. And in one or two instances I shall contravene completely what my colleagues, past and present, have written, but not without attempting to justify such drastic action.

One more thing: In what follows, Aboriginal 'tribal' names should not be taken too seriously. The first anthropologist to study the Aboriginal peoples of north-east Arnhem Land called them 'Murngin' (Warner, 1930-31, 1937), but this in fact is a name for a certain subgroup of the 'tribe'. So is 'Wulamba', used by a subsequent ethnographer (Berndt, 1955). I suppose I have not helped matters by calling them 'Miwuyt' (Shapiro, 1969a), but this at least is actually applied to the 'tribe' as a whole, though not by its own members: it means 'north-east', and is used for the Miwuyt (or Murngin or Wulamba) by—who else?—peoples to their south-west. And since it is less cumbersome than 'north-east Arnhem Landers', I shall use it here.

One might well ask how the Miwuyt talk about themselves. They call themselves *yulngu*, in contrast to *balanda*, which is applied to Europeans like myself. But they also apply *yulngu* to Aborigines outside north-east Arnhem Land, to Africans, and to Afro-Americans, whose photographs they see in periodicals. It hardly seems implausible that *yulngu* means 'dark-skinned person'.[2]

Now the Miwuyt know that beyond their borders customs are different. But these borders are not very sharply defined, and customs (as well as people) have crossed them with ease. So the Miwuyt, good social scientists that they are, conceive of ethnic differences in terms of relative location (e.g. 'south-western people', 'people living very far off'), absolute location ('coastal people', 'inland people'), and, nowadays, race. And they are not

---

[2] Like ourselves, the Miwuyt are much impressed by skin colour. The prosaic fact, however, is that Aboriginal Australians constitute a distinct race: they are not genetically related to Africans or Afro-Americans.

alone among Aborigines in this respect—though in parts of the continent native ethnological notions do seem to resemble the popular European fantasy of discrete tribes. I shall subscribe to this fantasy here to the extent that it makes labelling easier (where the anthropologist or the Aborigines have provided such labels); but you ought to remember that what we are dealing with is a batch of overlapping social and cultural fields, or, in certain senses, a single such field.

ONE

Ideologies of parenthood

A consideration of Aboriginal Australian kinship can begin, naturally enough, with native ideologies of parenthood. These have inspired an astonishing amount and tenor of controversy in the anthropological literature, so we had best begin with the only thing everybody (including anthropologists) agrees everybody (including Aborigines) agrees on: that women get impregnated, carry foetuses, and have and nurse babies. The Miwuyt, for example, express the relationship between an individual (call him X) and his mother (M) by a number of linguistic forms, among them the following:

> X is from M
> X is M's abdomen
> X is from M's abdomen
> M is the carrier of X
> X is the carried one of M
> M is X's nipples
> X is from M's nipples
> X is M's baby

These are translations of Miwuyt expressions, but even the more metaphorical of them surely seem 'natural' enough to Europeans. But now the delicate question: How does the woman get impregnated? Apparently most anthropologists who have posed this question to Aborigines have been told most of the time that the job gets done by a spiritual being, who enters the woman and is eventually incarnated as her child. This sounds a bit like the doctrine of the Virgin Birth, with the important difference that the 'miracle' happens all the time.

But then how does paternity figure in all this? Not, it would appear, very importantly—if indeed it can be said to figure in it at all! For reasons to be detailed in chapter 2, the spirit-child has to reveal certain attributes of itself, and it usually picks the husband of the child's mother for this revelation. But not always.

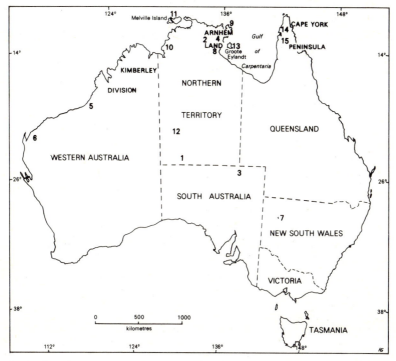

Australia, showing approximate location of tribes mentioned in the text
1 Arunta; 2 Dalabon; 3 Dieri; 4 Gidjingali; 5 Karadjeri; 6 Kariera;
7 Maljangaba; 8 Mara; 9 Miwuyt; 10 Murinbata; 11 Tiwi;
12 Walbiri; 13 Wanindiljaugwa; 14 Wikmunkan; 15 Yir-Yiront

Sometimes it chooses another man (who is not thereby suspected of carrying on with the mother) or a woman: in some tribes this may be the mother herself, who, it seems, can thus carry out her reproductive role untouched by human hands.

In north-east Arnhem Land (and many other parts of Australia) the spirit-child first manifests itself by mystically causing an unexpected event, most often an unusual abundance of a certain foodstuff. Its next appearance, where it conveys the information alluded to above, is in a dream, and the dreamer is most commonly the mother's husband. The latter exchanges this news for the whereabouts of his wife: these are curiously unknown to the spirit-child, even when the good woman is lying just beside her husband. Its deal completed, the spirit-child departs for lusher surroundings, thence to emerge in fleshly form in nine months' time. The mother's husband, meanwhile, consciously conveys this new information to his peers, once he is certain his wife has a bellyfull.

Hence a Miwuyt refers to his father as his 'finder'—that is the one who encountered him in spirit form. A father, conversely, refers to his child as 'one whom I found'.

Facts like these have led some commentators to argue that Aborigines are unaware of a connection between sexual relations and childbirth, that they are ignorant of physical paternity. The evidence for this position was first examined by Ashley Montagu (1937) and more recently by Spiro (1968), in a series of exchanges in the British journal *Man*. But other ethnographers have reported that the Aborigines are indeed aware of the facts of life.

One way out of this dilemma is to embrace both horns and say that some tribes are while others are not, which seems, after all, plausible enough. Another is to insist that the tribes that are have learned the facts from Europeans and other non-Aborigines, as some anthropologists have argued (Rose, 1968, p. 200; Stanner, 1933b, pp. 27-8). But this is a bit too easy, and it does injustice to what more careful ethnography has shown to be a remarkable subtlety in Aboriginal thought. Consider the following, the first pertaining to the Walbiri of Central Australia (Map 1), the second to the Miwuyt:

> . . . the Aborigines' answers to questions about conception depend on who is asked and in what circumstances. In ritual contexts, men speak of the action of the [spirit-child] as the significant factor; in secular contexts, they nominate both the [spirit-child] and sexual intercourse. The women, having few ritual attitudes, generally emphasize copulation (Meggitt, 1962, p. 273).

An occasion arose in which I could inquire directly of certain old men just what the semen did when it entered the uterus of a woman. They all looked at me with much contempt for my ignorance and informed me that 'that was what made babies'. I had not been able to obtain this information earlier because the ordinary savage [*sic*] is far more interested in the child's spiritual conception . . . than he is in the physiological mechanism of conception. . . . The relationship between the primitive men of north-eastern Arnhem Land and me as a field worker would be the same as that between the colonial Puritans of Massachusetts and the traditional visitor from Mars. Had the latter asked Cotton Mather or any other member of the community 'where babies come from', he would have discovered that they came from heaven, that God sent them . . . He would have been told this for approximately the same reason that the ordinary anthropological field investigator is informed by the natives that the totemic spirit is what causes impregnation (Warner, 1937, pp. 23-4).

These excerpts, I think, begin to place Aboriginal notions of conception into proper—and remarkably familiar—perspective: they entail a religious dogma (Leach, 1966), an 'ignoring', rather than an 'ignorance', of physical paternity. But they entail more than this.

My own Miwuyt informants (one of whom, by the way, is a son of Warner's best informant) were similarly aware—and at the same time deliberately 'unaware'—of the facts of life. What is more, their 'awareness' varied in a manner much the same as that of Meggitt's Walbiri. This came out in several situations, but perhaps most clearly when I recorded genealogies.

In some interviews I was concerned only to record the names of an informant's own children. (My genealogies were obtained from male informants.) The response usually took the form of the man's naming the first wife he acquired—Aborigines are polygynous—, followed by the children she bore him, in the order of their birth, then his second wife and her children, in proper birth-order, and so on. The following is a translated example:

First I acquired W_1 [name of first wife], and we began to copulate. A [name of first child] resulted from this. Then we copulated some more, and B resulted from this. Then we copulated more, and C resulted. Alright. Then I acquired W_2, and we began to copulate. D resulted from this. Then we copulated some more, and E resulted from this. . . . And that's all!

No 'ignorance' here— or 'ignoring' either! Not even a hint of spirituality. But when these same men were asked, on other occasions, to provide ritual lodge genealogies, they assumed a starkly contrasting piety. I shall have more to say about ritual lodges later. For the moment it need only be noted that they have to do with ceremonial life; and that among the Miwuyt and most other Aborigines they are *exogamous*—one may not marry another of his own lodge—and *patrilineal*: a child belongs to the lodge of his father. With that mouthful of information gulped down, we can look more intelligently at the genealogy given by a Miwuyt man of his ritual lodge:

I was the first one found by A [name of his father]. Then A found B, C, and D [names of the informant's siblings, in order of their birth].[1] A himself was found by E [name of the informant's paternal grandfather]. E also found F, G, and H [names of the informant's paternal aunts and uncles, in birth-order]. E himself was found by J [name of the informant's father's father's father]. But I never saw J, and I don't know whom he found besides E. He lived a long time ago!

Subsequent inquiry elicited the names of children of (for example) F and other male members of the lodge, to many of whom my informant could not relate himself by precise genealogical ties. Female lodge-members were named only as descendants: their own children, recall, were 'found' by men of other lodges, and the relationship of these children to their mothers' lodge is of a very different kind (chap. 4).

If you are as religious as my Aboriginal friends, this sort of genealogical reckoning should strike a familiar note. In fact, if we change some of its sequences so that sons invariably succeed

---

[1] The names of all his siblings were given, but those of his sisters were mentioned in a whisper and with eyes downcast. A Miwuyt man is not supposed to utter the names of his sisters and certain other relatives. This informant clearly compromised the prohibition, in response to my own insensitivity.

their fathers, and substitute 'begat' for 'found', it looks very much like many a Biblical genealogy. Most conspicuous in the two traditions is the second-class status of females—either considered only as descendants (Miwuyt), or only as immediate ancestors (Matthew 1:2-16), or excluded altogether (Genesis 10: 1-32). And if such poetic prose were the only information we had on the Aboriginal Australians and the Ancient Semites, we might be led to suspect that both peoples are or were ignorant of physical maternity.

This possibility may seem a bit incredible. There *are* cultures, however, that have the dogma that, although children undeniably emerge from women, the latter are rather like incubators: they house the developing foetus but do not contribute to its substance (Ashley Montagu, 1941; for a discussion of conception dogma, see Leach, 1961c, ch. 1 and Scheffler, 1973b, pp. 749-51). Anyway, we *do* know more about Aborigines (not to mention the Ancient Semites)—enough to say that the kind of genealogical reckoning noted above indicates, again, an 'ignoring' rather than an 'ignorance'—this time of physical *ma*ternity.

But why this ignoring? I would call attention to the following. The Ancient Semites had patrilineal kin-groups, as do the Aborigines, and in the perpetuation of such groups women are in an awkward position. Their reproductive powers are naturally essential, but these powers cannot be directly engaged by their brothers. They are used instead by men of other groups, and the products belong to these foreign—and thus eminently 'ignorable'—groups.[2]

This still leaves unanswered the question: Why, in certain contexts, did the Ancient Semites ignore only physical *ma*ternity, while the Aborigines have gone one better and pretended that physical *pa*ternity does not exist either? Here, I think, we have to avoid being dazzled by the popular term 'patrilineal' and look at a profound difference in kin-grouping between the two

---

[2] It is not, however, true that all cultures with patrilineal groups ignore or minimize maternity in their genealogical reckoning; but I suspect (to turn this around) that all cultures which ignore or minimize maternity in this way have patrilineal groups. It might be noted here that such groups among Ancient and many modern Semitic peoples are not entirely exogamous (Murphy and Kasdan, 1959).

cultures. This difference can be concisely put. Patrilineal groups among the Ancient Semites were internally differentiated by means of genealogical reckoning, whereas patrilineal groups in Aboriginal Australia are not internally differentiated at all.

Suppose we focus on two men in Biblical Israel. Let us say they are fourth cousins related through a sequence of males—which means they have the same father's father's father's father's father. For certain purposes they will use this fact to justify mutual support or common action. But on other occasions they might find themselves split or even mutually antagonistic, and this too could be justified genealogically: after all, they are not brothers, or even first cousins.

Now suppose we move these two men in time and space to Aboriginal Australia. Here their genealogical relationship is probably no more than a fact of biology; it is unlikely that they are even aware of it, and even if they are it would not be used to rationalize a co-operative endeavour. What they *will* know and employ is the fact that they are members of the same ritual lodge, and they are members of this group because their fathers are. If, on the other hand, they do not get along, they could avoid each other; but they have no way to idiomize their estrangement through patrilineal kinship.

This accounts for the limited genealogical memory of the second informant I quoted. It also makes intelligible the ignoring of physical paternity: if a ritual lodge is undivided into sub-groups, if all its members are always and forever 'brothers' of a kind, then their separate fatherhood is to that extent an awkward and disposable fact. This can perhaps be appreciated as a more durable version of the pose sometimes struck by us and other Semitically-inspired folk that we are all children of God.[3]

But this 'collectivist' theory of personality, when applied to the contingencies of human existence, must grapple with three problems. Two of these involve the communication of information: from the sacred world to the mundane world, concerning such things as the locale from which the spirit-child has

---

[3] Cf. the quote from Warner (1937) above. But not all cultures with genealogically undifferentiated kin-groups ignore physical paternity; nor is the converse true.

come (a factor whose importance will emerge in the next chapter); and, in the other direction, the woman to whom it should go in order to become incarnated. Aborigines have dealt with both in a single stroke—the 'finding' experience, which, when viewed from this angle, need not involve the father at all. But there is a third problem, one involving a kind of 'conflict' of information flowing in the sacred-to-mundane direction, and it is here that the father emerges as the 'finder' *par excellence*. To appreciate this we have to take a closer look at the ritual lodges.

TWO

Ritual lodges

I have mentioned in passing Aboriginal creation myths, noting that these stories, together with ceremonies in which they are re-enacted or otherwise represented, are owned by certain groups. These groups are the ritual lodges. The myths alluded to have several common elements, of which the following need to be noted here:

First, the myths involve the movement, within and usually beyond the tribal lands, of superhuman beings, who possess cultural and natural creative power.

Second, both spirit-children and certain natural features of the landscape were created by these beings, as their emanations or derivatives (cf. Genesis 1: 2, 27, 2: 7).

Third, the landscape was further divided by these beings through the magic of naming (cf. Genesis 1: 5, 8, 10), thus creating at least nominally distinct units. Following Stanner (1965), I shall call these units 'estates'.

Fourth, each of these estates, with its share of natural features, spirit-children and other emanations, and a narration of the doings of the superhuman beings while moving over it, were entrusted to human males. These were to pass this heritage on to males and, in a much more limited way, females of succeeding generations. Hence the origin of ritual lodges.

Now the estates thus created sometimes have natural boundaries such as rivers or hills, but not precise cultural boundaries. Probably the most common arrangement is a core area consisting of one or more sacred sites—natural features associated, in the manner just noted, with mythical beings—surrounded by land whose identity is increasingly uncertain with distance from the core. At its peripheries such an estate is all but indistinguishable from lands associated with other ritual lodges (Piddington, 1971; Pink, 1936; Stanner, 1965).

I have said that the ritual lodges are patrilineal: this is in fact somewhat of a simplification. In some regions an individual's lodge membership depends, according to native theory, not on his father's, but on more fortuitous circumstances, such as the locale in which he was born, or (probably more common) the one in which he was supposedly conceived. Affiliation here is to the ritual lodge associated with the relevant locale, which may or may not be the father's lodge. Hence the importance, at least in these regions, of that part of the 'finding' experience in which the spirit-child reveals its source (p. 23).

A. P. Elkin (1932a, p. 130, 1932b, p. 331) has gone so far as to suggest that these 'fortuitous' principles of recruitment are basic to ritual lodges; and that patrilineality is largely a response to depopulation of traditional lands and the concentration of Aborigines on mission and government settlements. Under these new conditions, presumably, 'fortuitous' principles lose their meaning: by them, instead of a tribe divided into several dozen lodges,[1] only one or two would eventually come to have any living members at all, and the bulk of the ritual heritage would go unattended. The way out of this dilemma is to minimize the importance of the 'finding' experience, simply by assigning each child as it is born to its father's lodge.

But why the father's? Elkin (1932a, pp. 129-30) believes that in pre-European times Aboriginal men usually lived on their lodge estates with their wives; that their children were conceived and born there; and that the lodges were therefore patrilineal anyway, if only 'on the ground'. The alleged adjustment would

---

[1] This vague estimate probably fits most tribes. Thus Warner (1937, pp. 39-51) lists forty-three Miwuyt lodges, Webb (1933, p. 409) fifty-one, and I have data on at least sixty. Meggitt (1962, p. 206) estimates 'some 30 or 40 separate lodges' for the Walbiri, while Sharp (1934, p. 20) gives a figure of twenty-eight for the Yir-Yiront of Cape York. Some of Elkin's figures for various tribes of the Kimberley Division are about the same as these, though others are much lower, reflecting in at least some cases a general depopulation of parts of the area (Elkin, 1933b, pp. 271-8, 1933c, pp. 437-8, 452, 471-3; Map 1).

thus have entailed nothing more drastic than an elevation of this situation to the cerebral level. But, as we shall see, Elkin's view of traditional Aboriginal residence grouping is at least questionable and probably false. More, although no anthropologist can claim to be the first European seen by a group of Aborigines, some have not been far behind; and their findings do not square at all with Elkin's hypothesis. Thus Lloyd Warner's fieldwork was begun only eight years after the arrival of missionaries in north-east Arnhem Land, yet the lodges he encountered were unequivocally patrilineal (Warner, 1937, pp. 16-29, 39-51, 68-9). T. T. Webb, an early missionary in the area, also writes of the 'patrilineal descent' of the lodges (1933, p. 406). In the vast desert regions of Western Australia (Map 1), where there are still Aborigines who have had minimal contact with Europeans, patrilineality has been reported by several observers (e.g. Berndt, 1959, pp. 96-104, 1972, pp. 189-93; Gould, 1969, p. 109; Tindale, 1972, pp. 223-7; Yengoyan, 1970, pp. 82-3). It is possible that these findings reflect 'overnight' processes stimulated by European contact, but only, I suspect, if such processes had a traditional base.

Let me elucidate my own position. I believe (though I cannot prove) that the use of 'fortuitous' principles to assign people to ritual lodges was at one time general in Australia: here I agree with Elkin. But I also believe that very early in the game, long before the coming of Europeans, men more or less deliberately and regularly attempted to play with these 'basic' rules, in such a way as to ensure that their children, especially their sons, wound up in the father's lodge. In most areas this could be done easily—for example, by rigging the 'finding' experience so that it occurs on the father's lodge estate, even when conception actually takes place elsewhere, or by somehow limiting the number of estates from which spirit-children can come, as has been reported (e.g. Berndt, 1959, p. 99; Elkin, 1933a, pp. 69-70; Sharp, 1934, p. 24). Where 'finding' is normally done by the mother rather than the father, manipulation of this sort would seem to be more difficult, but it appears nonetheless to occur (Pink, 1936, p. 290). In any case, I further believe that its

consistent practice eventually led in some areas to strict patrilineality and the collapse of 'finding' as a means of social
classification; in others to a less rigorously applied patrilineality
and a greater emphasis on the classificatory aspect of 'finding';
and that in a few areas 'finding' has retained its ancient appearance while its manipulation has gone formally unrecognized.

So while the resettlement wrought by Europeans probably
encouraged these processes, I do not think it initiated them: this
is no more than Elkin's most recent statement on the issue (Elkin,
1964, pp. 144-7).[2] Such a conclusion is not entirely conjectural.
It has substantial if indirect support in the literature on Aboriginal Australia (Berndt, 1959, p. 96; Elkin, 1933b, pp. 266-9,
1934, pp. 172-6; Stanner, 1936b, pp. 447-8; Strehlow, 1947, pp.
133-7); from an even more substantial amount of ethnographic
material—summarized by Schneider (1961, pp. 18-25)—on
simple societies outside Australia, indicating that, where fathers
are theoretically denied control over certain aspects of their
children's lives, they are nonetheless keen to have it anyway; and
from a body of data in social psychology which suggests that
regular 'subinstitutional' manoeuvers of this sort give rise, under
certain conditions, to a new institutional order which recognizes
them (Homans, 1961, esp. pp. 378-98). I cannot explain why
fathers are so ambitious, but here it need only be taken for
granted. We shall see later that this ambition emerges in another
sphere of Aboriginal life: the bestowal of their daughters in
marriage.

From now on I shall treat ritual lodges as patrilineal groups
everywhere in Australia. You might remember that this is a
simplification, but not, I think, too drastic a one.

Earlier I mentioned that Aboriginal creation myths involve
extensive movements through tribal lands by superhuman
beings. Ritual lodges whose estates were thus traversed by the
same mythical being share the ceremonial heritage associated
with that being. In most tribes lodges linked in this fashion may
not intermarry.

[2] Cf. Elkin (1963, p. 107): 'Whatever Aboriginal fathers long ago felt about it, all I have
known have laid very great . . . stress on their sons inheriting and learning the ritual which
they in their turn inherited and learnt.'

I have noted that lodge estates usually consist of a sacred core area surrounded by vaguely demarcated mundane land. Lodge ownership of the core area is unequivocal and behaviourally significant: admission of outsiders, along with revelation of the associated ritual heritage, is the greatest gift one man can bestow upon another, while entry by women or unauthorized men usually means death. According to much of the literature a similar exclusiveness attaches to the surrounding mundane area, but I refuse to believe this. I cannot see how such a state of affairs could exist when these lands lack, as they usually do, definite boundaries, nor is it plausible in view of what is now known about the composition of Aboriginal residence groups. Which brings us to another controversial topic.

THREE

Residence groups

Advocates of one side of the controversy maintain that, upon marriage, an Aboriginal man usually takes his wife to live with him on his lodge estate. This, as I have said, is A. P. Elkin's position, although Elkin, at least, has called attention to tribes with other residential norms (Elkin, 1950, pp. 17-18, 1953, pp. 417-18). A less compromising stance was taken by Radcliffe-Brown, and it is his name, and his outdated monograph *The social organization of Australian tribes* (1931), which are most commonly cited in this connection. Here is the crux of what Radcliffe-Brown had to say about Aboriginal residential grouping:

> . . . the important local group throughout Australia is what will here be spoken of as the *horde*. . . . Membership of a horde is determined in the first place by descent, children belonging to the horde of their father. . . . male members enter the horde by birth and remain in it till death. . . . The woman, at marriage, leaves her horde and joins that of her husband (1931, p. 4; emphasis in original).

Radcliffe-Brown's 'horde' is, in its composition, something like a ritual lodge, the systematic difference being that residential moves change the membership of the former but not the latter. We can ignore this scholastic distinction,[1] however, and focus

---

[1] Radcliffe-Brown also spoke of a patrilineal 'clan' which is 'connected with each horde'. 'The clan has all its male members in one horde, but all its older female members are in other hordes' (ibid., p. 28)—because of the supposed residential shift entailed by marriage. It is the clan, then, which is precisely identical with the ritual lodge, and which is a reality in Aboriginal social life; whereas the 'horde', as I hope to show, is a figment

instead on the substantial allegation: 'The woman, at marriage, leaves her horde and joins that of her husband.'

This is what some anthropologists call *patrilocal* residence. They contrast this with the custom whereby a man, at marriage, leaves his original residence group and joins that of his wife (*matrilocal* residence); and with the establishment by the married couple of a separate residence group apart from both sets of parents (*neolocal* residence), as is the norm in our own culture. Any student of the classics will know that the first two of these residential labels are a bit misleading (Adam, 1947), but this need not bother us much. More substantial matters, however, are these. Does 'patrilocal' here refer to a rule or to a statistical pattern or to both? If it refers to a rule, is the rule actually idiomized by the natives in terms of a residential shift at marriage, and in terms of co-residence with particular relatives (Goodenough, 1956)?

Peasants in parts of Ceylon—to take an example far removed from our geographic concern—recognize both patrilocal and matrilocal residence, have terms for both, and regard the former as preferable (Leach, 1961b, pp. 81-8): these people are in fact one of the few to which we can definitely attribute, according to the ethnographic literature, a rule of patrilocal residence. I do not think there is anything comparable in the literature on Aboriginal Australia. Here one encounters the notion that a man should die on his lodge estate (Peterson 1970b, 1972), a residence rule which has nothing to do with marriage or co-residence—and which, by the way, also argues against patrilocality as a statistical pattern.

Another non-Australian example will prove instructive. The Shavante Indians of Brazil have patrilineal groups like Aboriginal ritual lodges, but a matrilocal rule of residence. This rule by itself would have the effect of scattering the males of a patrilineal group, since each, at marriage, would go off to his wife's parental

of Radcliffe-Brown's very active imagination. Incidentally, in anthropology the term 'clan' is widely used for patrilineal groups like Aboriginal ritual lodges, for matrilineal groups (examples of which are discussed in the next chapter), but not, as in everyday English, for the sort of kinship categories also called 'kin', 'relatives', 'family', etc.

abode. But this scattering effect is counteracted by another rule: that patrilineally-related males should marry patrilineally-related females and thus stick together throughout life (Maybury-Lewis, 1967, pp. 96-104). Shavante residence groups thus look very much like Aboriginal 'hordes' are supposed to look—though they are generated by rules quite different from those intimated by Radcliffe-Brown.

These examples stress the utility of distinguishing between rules and statistical patterns in residence. They are of interest to those of us who, like myself, give 'people's concepts, standards, criteria, and principles for acting' priority over 'events and their statistical patterns' in ethnography (Goodenough, 1969, p. 329). Those of you who are more interested in the latter might look at two critical reviews of the data on Aboriginal residence groups: Hiatt (1962) concludes, on the basis of these materials, that the Radcliffe-Brown model does not hold on the ground, that most of the groups studied contain men of several ritual lodges. Birdsell (1970) takes the easy way out, arguing that the data reviewed by Hiatt should be ignored because they pertain to tribes influenced by Europeans; and that, if we were somehow able to defy the laws of logic by contacting uncontacted Aborigines, we would find Radcliffe-Brown's patrilocal 'hordes' in crystalline form.

This is clearly not a very satisfactory state of affairs. Birdsell's position has no substantial support, even among the 'contaminated' Aborigines whose social life has been studied. And even the greater respect for the evidence shown by Hiatt permits only the negative conclusion that the Radcliffe-Brown model is probably unfounded.

But recent research in north-east Arnhem Land—by myself and my colleague Nicolas Peterson of The Australian National University—has provided deeper insight into Aboriginal residence grouping. Most of my work was carried out on a mission station—a fact which would presumably cause Birdsell immediately to dismiss the entire case. But I was more patient. I found that patrilineal kinsmen indeed want to live together, though not at all to the exclusion of other males; on the contrary, they want with them those men who have married their daughters and sisters, for example, and who are therefore obligated to maintain them with a never-ending flow of gifts and services (pp. 102 *et seq.*). These same patrilineal kinsmen, however, have somebody else's sisters and daughters, and are similarly indebted to *their* wife-givers. A man, in short, is subject to two residential pressures, which (for added effect) might be called 'lodgemate love' and 'girl-giver greed'; it should now be clear that only the first reached Radcliffe-Brown's consciousness. When the two pressures come into conflict in a residence decision (as they usually do), the second, I found, nearly always takes priority.

But there are ways of eliminating this conflict. The most obvious is not to marry, which may for much of his life be the fate of an Aboriginal man (pp. 83-5) though not his choice. Another is to have one's lodgemate as an affine. Now this lodgemate/affine could not be a father- or brother-in-law, because of lodge exogamy. But it could be, for example, a mother-in-law and her brother. (If your wife's maternal uncle is not very important to you, it is because you are not an Aboriginal Australian.) Thus a man of a Miwuyt lodge called Bilkili cannot marry a Bilkili girl and so could not have a Bilkili father-in-law. But he could marry, for example, a Guyula girl whose father might have a Bilkili wife, who might have a brother. If you find this perplexing, know that it bothers the Miwuyt even more, though they tolerate it. I shall have more to say later about this sort of situation, in which mother-in-law and son-in-law are lodgemates, and why Aborigines try to avoid it.

The most common solution, however, to the residence dilemma, as well as the one most favoured, is the Shavante practice noted above: marry girls who are lodgemates to men who are lodgemates, and who can thus enjoy each other's company while being exploited by their common affines. This can not be considered matrilocal residence, though, because the question of who moves is irrelevant. Miwuyt mothers-in-law, in fact, are among the most mobile of creatures, and are quite prepared to settle in with their sons-in-law in order the better to get what is owed them.

I found these same values and patterns among Miwuyt living a more traditional life away from the mission station, which makes it difficult to explain them away as the results of European influence. But I still was not fully convinced.

Recall that, according to the Radcliffe-Brown model, male lodgemates not only live together throughout life; they live together on their lodge-estate. Now this is certainly not usually so in north-east Arnhem Land today, even among those living away from the mission station. But it could have been the case before the coming of Europeans, the effective date of which here is about 1920. To the extent that this was so, note carefully, men around that time would have been 'finding' their children in their own lodge-estates. This in turn implies that the conception-estate and lodge-estate of an individual about fifty or older at the time of my fieldwork would usually be the same. My data suggest that this was *not* usually so, that 'finding' was 'foreign'-based in at least half the relevant instances. And with that I rest my case (Shapiro, 1973).

Peterson's analysis (1970b) is restricted to a single band located to the west of the groups I studied. His direct findings are similar to mine; but of more interest are his inferences concerning the 'developmental cycle' of Aboriginal residence groups—how their composition changes over time, in regular fashion, through the values held by individuals and the opportunities open to them at several points in their lives. He suggests, following Radcliffe-Brown, that a man begins his career on his own lodge-estate. With marriage, however, he becomes obligated to his wife's parents, and, in order to serve them, he moves to the estate of his father-in-law. (This is consistent with my own findings, though Peterson goes further than I would and argues unequivocally for matrilocal residence.) But this situation is not permanent: when, for example, the father-in-law dies, our man returns, with wife and children, to his own estate. Here he draws unto him obligated sons-in-law and is thus able eventually to retire from active economic life; and here, in the midst of his spiritual heritage, his career ends.

Regrettably, there is no direct evidence for this cycle. But it, and our more substantial findings on group composition, do point the way to a fuller appreciation of Aboriginal residence grouping than that afforded by Radcliffe-Brown's oversimple scheme and Hiatt's demolition job. Further, I believe (though I cannot prove it) that these findings apply generally in Aboriginal Australia. I therefore cannot see how ritual lodges could have exclusive rights to subsistence resources on their estates (Radcliffe-Brown, 1931, p. 4), nor how they could be fighting units (ibid., p. 6; cf. Hiatt, 1965, pp. 134-41); and there is already abundant evidence that they do not figure as groups in the politics of marriage (chap. 10). Rather, their sphere of activity is the sacred. And even here their piece of the action is shared with mythically-linked lodges (p. 19), and with individuals tied to them by those mundane beings, women.

FOUR

Matrilineal ties

Patrilineal groups exist in most if not all of Aboriginal Australia. By contrast, *matrilineal* groups—those in which mother and child are co-members—have a more limited distribution. Like their patrilineal counterparts, Aboriginal matrilineal groups are usually exogamous; but otherwise the two kinds of unit are conceptualized very differently and have for the most part to do with different matters.

We have seen that the patrilineal lodges are ritual groups, and that they are associated with 'finding' and other spiritual notions. The matrilineal groups, as Elkin (1964, pp. 91-5) would have it, are 'social', and are associated with physicalistic representations: in many regions, for example, each such group is symbolized by a distinct natural species which is idiomized as the 'flesh' of its human members: '... the patrilineal principle is an expression of the belief in local spirit-centres and the doctrine of pre-existence and the "finding" of the spirit child, whereas the matrilineal principle is physiological in character ...' (ibid., p. 92).

Elkin's diagnosis of matrilineal groups as 'social' is elucidated by Jane Goodale's account of matri-sibs among the Tiwi of Melville Island (Map 1):[1]

> Members of a matrilineal sib assume a common line of descent through women of the sib. They do not and cannot trace their exact relationship to an ancestress, and, in fact, it does not appear important even to acknowledge a common ancestress; rather, the

[1] In anthropology 'sib' and 'clan' are usually employed synonymously (see note p. 21 n. 1).

importance lies in the assumed close relation . . . that members . . . acknowledge . . . Loyalty, cooperation, and mutual aid may be invoked . . .

Sib members are expected to help each other . . . by giving food, military aid, and shelter (Goodale, 1971, pp. 76-7).

It is worth noting that the Tiwi (ibid., p. 98) and many other cultures—both within and outside Australia—have both patrilineal and matrilineal groups: every individual in these societies is a member of one group of each kind. This possibility, which should be obvious, is often obscured by the pedantic application of the terms 'patrilineal' and 'matrilineal' to whole populations. This in turn carries the erroneous implication that the two sorts of group cannot exist in the same society.

In north-east Arnhem Land, by contrast, there are no matrilineal groups: individuals related through women do not constitute named or otherwise defined units whose membership acts collectively for some culturally recognized purpose. Nevertheless, a girl's matrilineal kin have primary rights over her bestowal in marriage, and they are categorized and treated in a distinct fashion by her potential husbands. I shall have more to say about this later; but it should be noted here that this is a very general state of affairs in Aboriginal Australia, both where matrilineal groups exist and where they are absent. There is thus a sort of conceptual division of labour in Aboriginal cultures, which may be expressed as follows: The *ritual* life of *males* is controlled by *spiritually* represented units (the lodges) in which membership is transmitted by *men*; whereas the *marital* life of *females* is controlled by *physicalistically* represented units ('flesh', concrete individuals) in which membership is transmitted by *women*. The Australian anthropologist Mervyn Meggitt has provided us with an elegant demonstration of this proposition for the Walbiri (Meggitt, 1972; see also Munn, 1973, pp. 213-21; Peterson, 1969). As for the ritual life of women and the marital life of men, we have already seen that the former is severely limited; and the latter, inasmuch as men are not generally objects of marital bestowal in Aboriginal Australia (pp. *95 et seq.*), is insignificant.

It is therefore possible to arrive at the following set of related dichotomies:

mundane world	sacred world
secular activities (e.g. marriage)	ritual activities
physicalistic representations	spiritual representations
women	men
matrilineal units	patrilineal units

This scheme would seem to distort reality, even culturally conceived reality. Thus, to take a single example, both men and women are in fact members of both patrilineal and matrilineal units; yet the scheme asserts that men are 'patri-creatures', women 'matri-creatures'. I believe, however, that although assertions like this are in one sense false, they are in another sense cultural exaggerations; and also, that their discovery does not have to wait for the intuition of a messianic analyst, but is based quite directly on specifiable ethnographic materials and procedures: I have indicated some of these above. I further believe that the scheme just presented gives an insight into Aboriginal social thought which is far more profound than an encyclopedic knowledge of ethnographic tidbits, and which squares with data we have for certain other cultures (Faris, 1969).

I cannot end this chapter without calling attention to one way by which this dichotomous scheme is, after a fashion, compromised: the role of *female* links in the ritual life of *males*. For generally in Aboriginal Australia, a man has important and distinctive relationships based not only on his own lodge membership, but on those of his mother and maternal grandmother as well.

In Miwuyt, most of the linguistic forms noted on p. 8, by which an individual's relationship to his mother is expressed, can also be employed to signify his tie with the mother's ritual lodge. Thus an individual whose mother's lodge is Bilkili (and who, because of lodge exogamy, could not himself be Bilkili) may be referred to as 'Bilkili's baby', and as being 'from Bilkili's abdomen'. More, the set of individuals whose mothers are of a single lodge—that set is distinguished by another linguistic form, and the male members of this category have special ritual obligations. During mortuary rites, certain foods are cooked in the middle of the ceremonial grounds, and these can be eaten only by men whose mothers are members of the lodge owning the rite. Another ritual prerogative of such men was first noted by Donald Thomson (1949, p. 26), who sojourned in the area shortly after Warner:

> The flesh of any kangaroo or other game which is killed with a spear or other weapon . . . which has been dedicated to a sacred clan totem, is also sacred, and may be eaten only by . . . the fully initiated members of the clan. On these occasions when the food or game is tabu, the division of the quarry is in the hands of . . . the men who apply the term *ngandi* (mother) . . . to the clan concerned . . . The . . . rights of these men take precedence even over those of the hunters who killed the quarry.

In some other parts of Australia, participants in rituals are divided into two categories, which anthropologists have seen fit to translate as 'owners' and 'managers'. Members of the former are the ceremonial actors, and they are of the lodge that owns the ritual; whereas the members of the latter category have the job of directing the actors, and they—the directors—seem usually to be sons of women of the owning lodge (Elkin, 1931b, pp. 58-9, 1934, pp. 176-80; Maddock, 1969a, pp. 21-3). This, incidentally, implies that a man is normally schooled in the ceremonial life not only of his own lodge but in that of his mother as well.

And his mother's mother's. But the maternal grandmother's lodge appears to loom less important in a man's ritual career. In north-east Arnhem Land I encountered distinctive terms for his tie to this group, and for the category of individuals matrilineally derived from it; but there seem to be no ritual obligations phrased exclusively in terms of this category. However, L. R. Hiatt of the University of Sydney, working among the Gidjingali, about 75 miles west of the Miwuyt (Map 1), found both distinctive terms and ceremonial acts (Hiatt, 1965, pp. 54-7).

FIVE

Moiety systems

The number of ritual lodges or matrilineal groups in an Aboriginal tribe does not seem especially important (see p. 26 n. 1), and there are several well-documented cases of particular groups of this kind dying out and of the relatively minor adjustments that ensue (Elkin, 1933b, pp. 285-7, 1934, p. 178; Pink, 1936, pp. 296-302; Strehlow, 1947, pp. 149-50). But the numerical aspect of certain other kinds of social unit appears to be more vital. The smallest possible number of units in such arrangements is of course two, in which case anthropologists speak of the units as constituting a *dual division* or, more frequently, a *moiety system*. Thus the two sex categories found in probably all cultures (Edgerton, 1964) can be considered a moiety system, and where this division is ritually elaborated, as in part of Australia, we might speak of 'sex moieties' (Radcliffe-Brown, 1952, p. 16; Elkin, 1964, p. 90). In fact very many schemes of social classification around the world are bipartite. My concern here, however, is with only two varieties, both of which occur widely in Australia and elsewhere. These have been named primarily by reference to the way in which they idiomize the choice of marital partners: 'exogamous moiety systems', in which an individual must marry (if he does marry at all) a member of the opposite moiety; and 'endogamous generation moieties', in which the appropriate spouse is a member of one's own unit (*endogamy* = 'marriage within').

Exogamous moiety systems are more common, and they raise more problems of theory. Among the Miwuyt and neighbouring tribes of Arnhem Land there is a scheme of this sort, whose components the Aborigines call Duwa and Yirritja (Warner,

1937, pp. 29-33; Elkin, 1950, pp. 15-16; Elkin, Berndt and Berndt, 1951; Hiatt, 1965; Maddock, 1969a). A Duwa man may marry only Yirritja women, a Yirritja man only Duwa women; offspring of marriages of the former kind are Duwa, of the latter Yirritja. These moieties are thus both exogamous and (apparently—but as we shall see, only apparently) patrilineal. Superficially they look like two ritual lodges writ large, and the lodges are indeed divided between the moieties. Hence not only is an individual's own lodge closed to him in his search for mates; so are the other lodges of his moiety.

Arrangements like these have led several anthropologists to speculate on the origin of exogamous moiety systems in connection with ritual lodges or lodge-like groups. Some have argued that the lodges came first, eventually coalescing into moieties; others reverse the process, arguing that moieties were the original form and that these gradually segmented into lodges. But most of the efforts on either side have been sheer guesswork. And, what is worse, the guessing has been based on a questionable premise: that an exogamous moiety system is simply a situation where two lodges, or super-lodges, happen to exist.

Most of our appreciation of Aboriginal moiety systems— exogamous and otherwise—derives from Radcliffe-Brown's 'The comparative method in social anthropology' (1952; see also Thomas, 1906, pp. 53-4, 68-9). In this article, Radcliffe-Brown called attention to the frequent use, in moiety names and other attributes, of systematically related pairs of categories:

> The Australian idea of what is here called 'opposition' is a particular application of that association by contrariety that is a universal feature of human thinking, so that we think by pairs of contraries, upwards and downwards, strong and weak, black and white. . . . In the tales about [the moiety eponyms] eaglehawk and crow the two birds are opponents in the sense of being antagonists. They are also contraries by reason of their difference of character, Eaglehawk the hunter, Crow the chief. Black cockatoo and white cockatoo, which represent the moieties in western Victoria, are another example of contrariety, [in this case through] the contrast of colour. [In some American Indian tribes] the moieties are referred to by other pairs of contraries, Heaven and Earth, war and

peace, up-stream and down-stream, red and white. . . .
wherever . . . there exists a social structure of exogamous moieties,
the moieties are thought of as being in a relation of what is here
called 'opposition' (Radcliffe-Brown, 1952, pp. 18-19).

Such 'social structures' are probably more accurately regarded
as classificatory schemes, by which natural forms and cultural
artifacts, as well as human beings, are ordered. Warner (1937,
pp. 30-1) saw this in the Duwa/Yirritja division in north-east
Arnhem Land:

> Everything in Murngin civilization is divided on this dual basis.
> There is nothing in the whole universe . . . that has not a place in
> one of the two categories. . . . allocation is made by an association
> that sometimes seems irrational to a European but is perfectly
> reasonable to the native mind. . . . the reasoning is as justifiable,
> granted the premise, as for our own classifications.
>
> To illustrate the principle: a red parrot is Dua because of his
> [mythical] association with the Dua creator women; red parrot
> feathers, one of the chief articles of decoration, are Dua because
> of this; baskets covered with red parrot feathers are Dua. The spear
> thrower is Dua, the sting-ray spear belongs to the same moiety, but
> the wooden spear is Yiritja. The shark belongs to the Dua moiety;
> the barramundi is Yiritja . . .
>
> The above association of objects may seem arbitrary. . . ., but
> every article fits into an elaborate ideological system which finds
> expression in myth and folklore. The white man is Yiritja, there-
> fore all of his culture is Yiritja; so that if a tin can is thrown away
> at a mission station the native who captures this valued prize
> knows that it is Yiritja . . . The white man is Yiritja because the
> Malay trader before him was Yiritja, and Malay and white man,
> to the native, are obviously alike.

Actually, even from this passage, it is far from clear in many
cases that moiety 'allocation is made by an association that . . .
is perfectly reasonable to the native mind'. Why, for example,
is the spear-thrower Duwa and the wooden spear Yirritja? There
may be stories, as Warner suggests, that account for this
assignment, but what accounts for the assignment of the stories?
On the basis of our present state of knowledge, probably all that
can be concluded is that these tales provide an irreducible basis

for classification according to a moiety scheme. And even where such arrangements seem grounded in a 'natural' opposition (Eaglehawk/Crow, Heaven/Earth, etc.), the assignment of particular items is very often no less arbitrary.

Moreover, although these classificatory schemes have, as noted, a global character, they handle people in a radically different fashion from everything else. Human beings are classed *specifically*, that is on an individual basis, so that some belong to one moiety, others to the other; whereas non-human beings, inanimate objects, etc. are classed *generically*, that is according to kind, so that, for example, in Miwuyt thought all spiders are Yirritja.[1]

Conventional behaviour carried out in a moiety idiom stresses complementarity and opposition. The confinement of an individual's erotic and marital partnerships, in exogamous moiety systems, to the opposite unit is only one expression of this theme, and should not be over-emphasized at the expense of others.[2] Among these in north-east Arnhem Land is the notion that in hunting, a man should avoid animals of his own moiety and seek as game only those of the other division.[3] Elsewhere in Australia, the 'owner'/'manager' ritual distinction has been reported

[1] There are some unimportant and readily understandable exceptions to this rule. Thus in north-east Arnhem Land, dogs—the only domesticated animals—are classed specifically. Incidentally, Warner's statement, quoted above, that 'The white man is Yiritja' (i.e. is classed generically), is ambiguous and suggests a non-existent racism on the part of the Miwuyt. The European as a category of being is indeed Yirritja, but individual Europeans, like individual Aboriginals, are classed specifically. I myself happen to be Duwa.

[2] The expression 'exogamous moieties' is not entirely appropriate, since it suggests that what we are dealing with are units of the ritual lodge order. I use it primarily to provide a basis for comparison, so that this notion can be dispelled. Following Radcliffe-Brown (1952) and Lévi-Strauss (1960), I suspect we can learn more about such arrangements by linking them instead to other bipartite classifications, many of which are neither exogamous nor, in the conventional sense, moiety systems. Examples of these classifications can be found on pp. 29 and 72 *et seq.* of this book, and in Hale (1971) and Munn (1964, 1969). Durkheim's ambitious and classic statement on Aboriginal dualism (1915) does not square with the available evidence (Stanner, 1967).

[3] This suggests a parallel in Aboriginal thought between killing (and perhaps eating) on the one hand and sexual intercourse on the other (McKnight, 1973). That this notion is not exclusively Australian property is suggested by a recent analysis by Leach (1964), and by a rather enormous mass of ethnography, including certain aspects of European folk

as being effected on a moiety basis, such that the 'owners' are members of the moiety in which the relevant ceremony is classed and the 'managers' members of the opposite moiety. I suspect, however, that this distinction is more commonly made on the basis of lodge affiliation, in the fashion indicated in the preceeding chapter. In any case, there are very many other examples of relational symbolism involving moieties. Elkin (1964, p. 97) provides a partial enumeration:

> In many tribes, the members of one moiety camp apart from the members of the other moiety, on opposite sides of a creek, for example, or on high ground and low ground respectively. . . . Ball games are . . . played in Victoria and the Gulf of Carpentaria country by moieties . . . in north-eastern South Australia, the members of one moiety have the privilege of 'killing' or initiating a youth of the other moiety . . .

In the ethnographic and theoretical literature, some exogamous moiety systems are characterized as matrilineal, the remainder as patrilineal. Evidence from north-east Arnhem Land, however, indicates that a third means of assigning membership exists.

Warner (1937, p. 31) took the Duwa/Yirritja scheme to be patrilineal, and there would seem to be substantial grounds for this conclusion: Duwa women almost always, it seems, get impregnated by Yirritja men, within or without wedlock, and the outcome is Yirritja; and when the job gets done to a Yirritja woman it is supposed invariably to be by her Duwa husband or lover, and the offspring is Duwa in either case. But what happens when people do not stick to the straight and narrow? Suppose, say, that a Duwa man were carrying on with a woman of his own moiety. Such a liaison could never end in marriage, but no matter: the children it might produce have to be placed in the moiety scheme, and Miwuyt law distinguishes between the child's (presumed) father and the mother's husband. So, since the father is Duwa, the children are Duwa. Right?

culture of which all but the most naive will be aware. See also Lévi-Strauss (1966, pp. 105-6, 1969b, p. 269).

Wrong. In the two instances of this very sort that came to my attention in the field, the children were assigned to Yirritja. Why? Because, I was told, the mothers are Duwa. The principle, then, appears to be, not the patrilineal one that an individual is assigned to the unit of his father, but one of another stripe, that moiety membership is matri-determined, though not matrilineal: assignment is to the moiety *opposite to* that of the mother. I inferred that this principle is in fact operative in all instances, though it is effectively different from patrilineality only in such unusual cases; and that for this reason it may be much more common ethnographically than we now believe (Shapiro, 1967a).

To those of you who think this is splitting hairs, I could point out that 'my' principle successfully 'predicts' *all* instances of moiety assignment in north-east Arnhem Land, whereas the patrilineal one is an effective winner only *most* of the time. But this will only convince you of my follicle fetish, and besides, I do not find much safety in numbers. I would prefer instead to return to the position I took in my discussion of Aboriginal residence groups and reiterate the priority of standards over statistics. I shall note too that the way the Miwuyt apparently reckon an individual's moiety membership is nothing but the application, in a sphere in which anthropologists have been blinded by the notion that a moiety is a large lodge, of an idea familiar elsewhere (pp. 65-7, 77).

Here, then, the very location of an individual within a system of social units is dependent on a unit other than his own. Add to this their classificatory character, and the sundry expressions of complementarity and opposition, and it becomes clear that moiety schemes are conceptual systems. 'Systems' of lodges and lodge-like units, by contrast, are more like arbitrary collections of people, and their systemic qualitites are much more limited. Lévi-Strauss (1966), following Durkheim and Mauss (1963, pp. 17-26), has argued against this conclusion, but the ethnographic evidence seems mostly to support it (Hiatt, 1969; Worsley, 1967).

Still, the contrast can be pushed too far. Lodges are not mobs: they have, as we have seen, legendary histories and rules of recruitment; and to some degree their relations with other lodges are ordered by exogamy and the distribution of ritual objects. In Aboriginal Australia they do not seem to approach the degree of systematization of moiety schemes, but this is not always true elsewhere. Thus the Bororo Indians of Brazil—linguistic cousins of the Shavante (p. 22)—are divided into eight matrilineal groups, each of which is supposed to be represented in every village of the tribe:

> The clans' positions in the village circle are localized with reference to the cardinal points as determined by the course of the sun, so that each clan stands in a defined geographical relation to every other clan. . . . In referring to any clan the Bororo customarily nod or gesture towards that point of the compass where that clan is supposed to lie. . . . *Each clan is seen as a totally unique and vital element in the social structure.* Each has a precise standing in the village circle which belongs to it alone, and members of one clan cannot be substituted for those of another. Every clan is associated with an established set of natural species, meteorological and geographical phenomena, cultural items and certain named spirits, and none of these appears in the set owned by any other clan (Crocker, 1969b, p. 46; emphases added).

The number of units in a systemic scheme can thus be greater than two: in chapter 7 we shall examine some Aboriginal illustrations of this proposition which look hardly at all like lodges. What I might suggest here is that the clan (lodge)/moiety distinction is less salient theoretically than the non-systemic/ systemic continuum.

My discussion has so far been couched in terms of exogamous moiety schemes. Most of what I have said is also germane to 'endogamous generation moieties', on which our best data come from Meggitt's study of Walbiri culture:

> The Walbiri . . . possess reciprocal terms for the . . . alternate generation levels. A man refers to all members of his own moiety as *jalbaru-gulangu*, 'equivalent status-belonging to'; *jalbaru* is also a male term of address and reference for age-mates. Members of the opposite moiety are *ngauwu-gulangu* or *guiju-gari*, 'flesh-having' (Meggitt, 1962, p. 189).

Note that an individual's *jalbaru-gulangu* include not only members of his own generation, but those of his grandparents and grandchildren as well; whereas those who are *ngauwu-gulangu* to him are of the parental and filial generations. This 'merging of alternate generations' is a very general principle in Aboriginal social classification, and we shall come across it again. Incidentally, the use of relational rather than absolute terms (like Duwa and Yirritja) is very common with all kinds of moiety system.

Since Radcliffe-Brown reminded us of the frequent association of exogamous moiety systems with opposed pairs of birds, we should not be too surprised to learn that one Walbiri generational division is linked to a species of eagle, the other to the pink cockatoo (ibid., p. 188). Similarly, the Walbiri units are bound by reciprocal services:

> The chief function of the endogamous moieties appears to concern the allocation of roles in the few ceremonial activities that are peculiar to women . . . women of each moiety possess in common a collection of decorative patterns, which they paint on their bodies for the dances. . . . It is the duty of an informally elected female leader to superintend the women of the opposite moiety as they paint the patterns . . . on the dancers of her own moiety . . . (ibid., pp. 189-90; cf. Munn, 1973, p. 14).

There is no evidence, however, that 'endogamous generation moieties' have the global classificatory character so frequently found with exogamous moiety systems. Further, at least among the Walbiri, the endogamous dual division 'is never invoked as a criterion of classification in discussions of marriage' (Meggitt, 1962, p. 189), although it is consistent with other categorical schemes which are so invoked (chapter 6).

Just as ritual lodges and matrilineal groups sometimes occur together, so a culture may contain both exogamous and endogamous moiety systems. The Walbiri, in fact, elaborate on this: Meggitt reports exogamous patrilineal moieties and exogamous matrilineal moieties, in addition to the endogamous division (1962, pp. 190-2, 203-4; see also Munn, 1973, pp. 13-15). Even more impressive expressions of the moiety principle have been reported from outside Australia (Nimuendajú and Lowie, 1937).

SIX

Relationship terminologies

I centred the preceeding section on a paper Radcliffe-Brown
published three years before his death. I begin this one with a
large dose from a much younger man, purveyed to the anthropological public when he was plain old A. R. Brown, unknown
but steadfast bearer of the White Man's Burden. Writing at a
time when the British Lion had not yet applied for dentures, he
had this to say about the Kariera of Western Australia (Map 1):

> Although *the use of the terms of relationship is based on actual
> relations of consanguinity and affinity, it is so extended as to
> embrace all persons* who come into social contact with one
> another. If we take any single member of the tribe, then every
> person with whom he has any social dealings whatever stands to
> him in one or other of the relations denoted by the terms . . . In this
> way *the whole society forms a body of relatives.* . . . a man or
> woman never addresses anyone, except young children, by a
> personal name, but uses the appropriate relationship term. . . . *The
> natives preserve their genealogies carefully in their memories,*
> though in these degenerate days the younger men and women
> neglect such knowledge. . . . When a stranger comes to a camp . . .
> he does not enter the camp, but remains at some distance. A few
> of the older men . . . approach him, and the first thing they proceed
> to do is to find out who the stranger is. . . . *The discussion proceeds
> on genealogical lines until all parties are satisfied of the exact
> relation of the stranger to each of the natives* present in the camp.
> When this point is reached, the stranger can be admitted to the
> camp . . . I took with me on my journey a native of the Talainji
> tribe, and at each native camp we came to, the same process had
> to be gone through. In one case, after a long discussion, they were
> still unable to discover any traceable relationship between my

servant and the men of the camp. That night my 'boy' refused to sleep in the native camp, as was his usual custom, and on talking to him I found that he was frightened. *These men were not his relatives, and they were therefore his enemies. . . . If I am a blackfellow and meet another blackfellow that other must be either my relative or my enemy* (Radcliffe-Brown, 1913, p. 150; emphases added).

It is impossible for a man to have any social relations with anyone who is not his relative because there is no standard by which two persons in this position can regulate their conduct towards one another. I am compelled to treat a person differently according as he is my 'brother', 'brother-in-law', 'father', or 'uncle' (ibid., p. 157; emphases added).

This would be merely a quaint piece of anthropological history, but for the embarrassing fact that all or parts of it have somehow come to be received wisdom about Aboriginals. I have underscored those portions that are contentious, misleading, or downright false—except, no doubt, for the 'degenerate' Kariera. These excerpts can, I think, reasonably be translated into the following set of assertions:

1) Aboriginal relationship terms are kinship terms—i.e. they are 'based on actual relations of consanguinity and affinity', and their application to the wider society thus involves a process of extension. This assertion, long taken for granted, has recently become part of a hotly contested issue, with fairly profound implications for anthropology at large. We had best postpone its consideration until I have said a bit more about Aboriginal relationship terminologies.

2) In Aboriginal Australian societies, everybody is a kinsman to everybody else: '. . . the whole society forms a body of relatives'. Note that this in no sense follows from the preceding assertion. Thus in our own society, we might call a clergyman 'father' or a co-member of a 'fraternal' order 'brother', but neither is (necessarily) a kinsman. Aboriginal approximations to these usages are considered below.

3) Detailed genealogical reckoning is employed in the application of relationship terms: 'The natives preserve their genealogies carefully in their memories . . .'. I have already

(p. 12) given some indication of the limited genealogical concern of Aboriginals. It would therefore seem unlikely that they bother themselves with their 'exact relation' to a newcomer. We have, in fact, good information, some of which is summarized below, on the principles they *do* use to classify others.

4) There is a dichotomy kinsman/enemy in Aboriginal languages: 'If I am a blackfellow and meet another blackfellow, that other must be either my relative or my enemy.' It is doubtful Radcliffe-Brown knew Kariera or any other native Australian tongue well enough to establish this, and I therefore consider it sheer romanticism. Aborigines classify *everyone* by means of relationship terminologies, but this does not preclude the existence and application of an 'enemy' category and the establishment of antagonistic relations.

5) Appropriate social relations are governed largely if not entirely by relationship category: 'I am compelled to treat a person differently according as he is my 'brother', 'brother-in-law', 'father', or 'uncle'. Actually, Radcliffe-Brown (1913, pp. 156-7) had a glimmer of the limitations, if not the absurdity, of this notion; but his failure to follow it up signalled an early stage in the paralysis of the anthropology of interpersonal relations. Drs Goodenough (1965) and Keesing (1969, 1970b), among a very few others, have shown how this malady can be more rigorously treated; but so far most of Australian Aboriginal anthropology has not got beyond the highly intuitive application of a Leach (1964)—or a Lévi-Strauss (1963, ch. 2; cf. Maddock, 1970b; McKnight, 1971, pp. 172-6, 1973; but see also Dixon, 1971; Hale, 1971). I return to this in chapter 10.

But if incorporation into the relationship scheme is no guarantee of amity and only a limited guide for behaviour, then why are the Aborigines so insistent on classifying people in this way? Sociologically-oriented anthropologists like to say that it 'provides a mechanism of social cohesion'; materialistically-oriented anthropologists like to say that it 'is a device for marshalling labor and guaranteeing efficient distribution of resources'; ethologically-oriented anthropologists like to say that this classificatory bent is 'in the wiring of the human animal and got there by mutation and natural selection'; and I should like to say that all of these statements are vacuous.[1] So maybe, following Lévi-Strauss (1966) and, in my view, the most important figure in the first half-century of professional anthropology in the United States, the late A. L. Kroeber (1952, ch. 26), we should just regard Aboriginal preoccupation with classification as a 'given'. We can thus proceed directly to an examination of its products, their internal logical principles, and the ramifications of these.

The most common (though not the most sophisticated) way of analysing relationship terminologies is to consider how they classify certain close kin, especially in the parental and one's own generations. This approach stems from Morgan (1871) but is nowadays most closely associated with the work of Murdock (1949, pp. 141-83, 223-59). Consider the following relatives: father, father's brother, mother's brother. In English we have a separate term for the first, but we lump the second and third under one term ('uncle'). This may seem natural, but in fact it is not done in the majority of human languages. In most Aboriginal Australian tongues father and his brother are called by the same term, which is different from the term applied to mother's brother.[2] For this pattern of classification we have the handy if self-contradictory rubric 'bifurcate merging' (Lowie, 1928).

Now consider these relatives: mother, mother's sister, father's sister. English separates the first from all others and merges the second and third ('aunt'). Naturally! Not really: most Aboriginal languages merge the first and second and apply a different term to the third. Again, bifurcate merging.

So much for the parental generation. Moving to one's own, we

---

[1] This is not the place to discuss the criteria for an adequate causal explanation, but I suspect that most of you who have been exposed to the social sciences may actually believe these statements say something. For why they do not, see Hempel (1965, esp. pp. 246-58, 297-330).

[2] Most analyses of relationship terminologies ignore the linguistic qualities of the terms themselves and consider only whether or not the same term is applied to two given relatives. Thanks largely to Leach (1967, 1971), it is now apparent that this tactic restricts our appreciation of these systems. I shall therefore use it here only when it does not appear to be limiting in this way.

can perhaps best appreciate part of both the English and Aboriginal patterns in terms of what has been called 'the rule of uniform descent':

> If somebody whom ego calls A has children whom ego calls B, then the children of everybody ego calls A are called B. Thus, in our society, the children of all uncles are 'cousins', the children of all brothers or sisters are called 'nephews' and 'nieces', etc. (Tax, 1937, p. 19).

'Ego', as you may have guessed, is the hypothetical individual from whose standpoint we are looking at the relationship terminology. As an Aboriginal Australian, he or she would thus apply the same term or terms to siblings, the children of the father's brother, and those of the mother's sister, by employing 'the rule of uniform descent'. Moreover, he or she would distinguish these relatives from the children of the mother's brother and those of the father's sister, through my own elaboration of this rule:

> If somebody whom Ego calls A has children whom Ego calls B, then the children of everybody Ego calls A are called B. Further, if somebody whom Ego does not call A but who is of the same sex as somebody Ego calls A—if such an individual has children—, then these children are not called B. Thus in English the children of all uncles are 'cousins', but the children of fathers are 'brothers' and 'sisters'.

Finally, by employing this elaboration, and taking account of the new information that, in Aboriginal cultures, the appropriate wife of the mother's brother is somebody in the relationship category which includes the father's sister, and the appropriate husband of the father's sister is somebody in the relationship category which includes the mother's brother, we can successfully 'predict' that the children of the mother's brother are classed with those of the father's sister.

Such bifurcate merging terminologies[3] probably always take

---

[3] In the strictest sense the expression 'bifurcate merging' pertains only to a pattern of kin-classification in the parental generation; the analogous pattern in Ego's generation is conventionally given another label (Murdock, 1949, pp. 223-4). I plead poetic licence.

account of a wider circle of people than the close kin we have
been considering, and it is now clear that even the genealogical
principles by which they do this are not everywhere the same
(Lounsbury, 1964; Scheffler, 1971a). This, however, need not
concern us here.

Another way of looking at relationship terminologies is by
examining the relations among the terms themselves, without
much regard to what they otherwise signify: this approach stems
from the British scholar A. M. Hocart (1937). If we do this, then
the terms applied to the medial three generations of relatives—those of Ego's generation, the parental, and the filial—in
most Aboriginal relationship terminologies can be simplified into
the following pattern:

'father'/'father's sister'	'mother'/'mother's brother'
'sibling'	'cousin'
'man's child'	'woman's child'

Here we should take the words enclosed by quotes to be
glosses: terms which, though they are applied to the particular
objects (in this case, relatives) they indicate, are applied to other
objects as well; and which should be regarded as no more than
convenient labels for foreign words, the better to talk about
these.

'Father'/'father's sister' and 'man's child' are reciprocals: if
you call me 'man's child', I call you 'father' or 'father's sister',
depending on your sex. The same relationship exists between
'mother'/'mother's brother' and 'woman's child'. 'Sibling',
however, is self-reciprocal: if you call me 'sibling', I call you
'sibling'. The same holds for 'cousin'. This last gloss, by the way,
is a bit misleading: among genealogical first cousins it is applied
only to the children of the mother's brother and those of the
father's sister. Those of the father's brother and those of the
mother's sister, you will recall, are in the 'sibling' category.

The glosses 'man's child' and 'woman's child' need some
explication too. In English and most other languages husband
and wife apply the same relationship term, or set of terms, to their
mutual offspring. In most Aboriginal languages, however, this
is not the case. Instead, the husband *and all his siblings* apply one

relationship term, or set of terms—'man's child'—to his off-spring, while the wife *and all her siblings* apply another term, or set of terms—'woman's child'—to these same offspring.

All this may seem strange. But it should help to assume—as is often so—that this terminological pattern occurs in cultures with an exogamous moiety system, like the Duwa/Yirritja division in Arnhem Land. A little playing around with close genealogical positions will suggest that each term classes relatives who are in only one moiety slot—same or opposite—with respect to Ego. A wider perspective gives the same results: the terms in the left-hand column are applied to own-moiety people, those in the right-hand column to opposite-moiety people. Not just to close relatives but to everybody, as we learned from Radcliffe-Brown (Shapiro, 1970a).

Some anthropologists who have noted the frequent occurrence of this terminological scheme with exogamous moiety systems have argued that the latter are older; and that historically they gave rise to the former. Where the scheme exists but the moieties do not, these same anthropologists usually assume they once did. But this is sheer speculation. I see no reason to assert any more than the evidence indicates: that the two fit the same mould.

If the two columns order the terms in accordance with an exogamous moiety structure, what orders the terms within each column? One answer is what some anthropologists like to call *patrifiliation*, which means nothing more than the father : child link. Thus the child of a 'father' is a 'sibling', and the child of a (male) 'sibling' is a 'man's child'; the child of a 'mother's brother' is a 'cousin', and the child of a (male) 'cousin' is a 'woman's child'. The Miwuyt refer to such links as 'following the father's path'.

The other answer is more commonly applied in Aboriginal Australia, and it is far more interesting. This is the *mother* : child link—*matrifiliation*—which the Miwuyt, as you might suspect, call 'following the mother's path'. Here we have to move our eyes a bit more: the child of a 'father's sister' is a 'cousin'; the child of a (female) 'cousin' is a 'man's child'; the child of a 'mother' is a 'sibling'; and the child of a (female) 'sibling' is a 'woman's child'. Note that this principle of ordering within a column appeals, as it were, to the other column—something reminiscent of the way the Miwuyt classify people in terms of their exogamous moiety division (p. 23).

This suggests that the terms are ordered not only by principles of moiety and filiation, but by marriage as well, and this is indeed the case. Thus the appropriate spouse of a 'father' is a 'mother'; of a 'father's sister' a 'mother's brother'; of a 'sibling' a 'cousin' (of the opposite sex); and of a 'man's child' a 'woman's child' (of the opposite sex). We can also correctly infer in-law relationships among the terms: e.g. the appropriate mother-in-law of a 'sibling' is a 'father's sister'. So important, in fact, are certain affinal relationships in Aboriginal Australia that the terminological pattern under consideration might well have been glossed as:

'father'/'mother-in-law'	'mother'/'father-in-law'
'sibling'	'spouse'
'woman's child-in-law'	'man's child-in-law'

But this is getting a bit ahead of the game. Let us instead return to my original representation of the pattern, this time taking account of the grandparental and grandchildren's generations. We then have:

'father's father'/ 'mother's mother'	'mother's father'/ 'father's mother'
'father'/'father's sister'	'mother'/'mother's brother'
'sibling'	'cousin'
'man's child'	'woman's child'
'man's son's child'	'woman's son's child'

Remember that these are glosses. In English we can distinguish, for example, the two kinds of grandmother by modifying terms ('maternal', 'father's side', etc.). In most Aboriginal languages, by contrast, such terms are unnecessary, since a distinction is made at the primary level of linguistic morphology. This should no longer be surprising, because it is just another expression of the exogamous moiety pattern.

Now in many Aboriginal languages the terms at the top and bottom of each column are not entirely distinct: often they sound alike, and in some cases the very same term suffices for both positions.[4] More, 'sibling' is frequently an acceptable alternative for people in both positions. There is thus a partial merging of alternate generations, a pattern we have encountered in more complete form in endogamous moiety schemes. This comes closer to fulfilment in some cultures, in which, under certain conditions, people in the 'father' and 'man's child' positions with respect to each other, or in the 'mother's brother' and 'woman's child' positions with respect to each other, apply to each other a single self-reciprocal term. Although probably no Aboriginal culture permits all of these mergings all the time, the realized pattern may be represented as follows:

'sibling'	'cousin'
'father'/'father's sister'	'mother'/'mother's brother'
'sibling'	'cousin'
'father/'father's sister'	'mother'/'mother's brother'
'sibling'	'cousin'

Several languages have terms which can be applied to people in the same position in *either* column. Elkin (1939, pp. 215-16, 1964, pp. 75-8) regards the resultant pattern as a distinct 'type', though it is clearly a situational and structural variant of what we have been considering so far. Its fulfilment is a perfect realization of the endogamous moiety pattern:

'sibling'
'father'/'mother'
'sibling'
'father'/'mother'
'sibling'

This terminological pattern, for obvious reasons, is often called 'generational'. Though it sometimes occurs separately, at least outside Australia, its co-existence with bifurcate merging has been established for non-Aboriginal cultures as well (Basso, 1970, 1973, pp. 78-81; Kaplan, 1972).

The Kariera relationship terminology is of the bifurcate

[4] In this paragraph and the next I rely heavily on the analyses of Harold Scheffler of Yale University (Scheffler, 1971b, 1972c, 1973a), though it is certain he would not advocate my representations.

merging sort, and several anthropologists, including Radcliffe-Brown (1913) and myself (Shapiro, 1970a), have taken it to be similar to the scheme just considered. A re-analysis by Goodenough (1970, pp. 131-42), however, indicates we are all wrong. In Kariera, as in English, husband and wife apply the same terms to their mutual offspring, while another set of terms is applied to these offspring by their parents' *opposite*-sex siblings—mother's brother and father's sister. Unlike English, though, and as in most other Aboriginal languages, parents' *same*-sex siblings—father's brother and mother's sister—use the same terms as parents.

What all this means here is that the foregoing representations will not fit Kariera, which may have a radically different structure. This structure can be represented as follows for the medial three generations:

'father'/'mother'	'mother's brother'/'father's sister'
'sibling'	'cousin'
'child'	'opposite-sex sibling's child'

Although this pattern occurs with an exogamous moiety system (Radcliffe-Brown, 1913, p. 159), it is not congruent with such a system: 'child', for example, is either an own- or an opposite-moiety term, depending on the sex of Ego. What, then, can we make of Kariera?

A little while ago, I made a half-hearted attempt to provide affinal glosses for part of our first terminological pattern. The same effort for Kariera yields something much more interesting:

'father'/'mother'	'father-in-law'/'mother-in-law'
'sibling'	'spouse'
'child'	'child-in-law'

The suggestion, then, is that the salient dichotomy in Kariera is not own-moiety people/opposite-moiety people, as with our first pattern; but rather kin/affines, or—more accurately—those with whom one may not contract affinal relationships/those with whom one may do so (cf. Dumont, 1957).

This analysis may seem too good to be true, and I really have no evidence that, for Kariera or any other Aboriginal culture, it is anything more than my own creation. But, as it happens, similar terminologies are very common elsewhere, and for some of these we have much better information. Perhaps the best is for the Ojibwa Indians of Canada, whose language recognizes my two columns by two cover-terms, which appear to mean something like 'relatives' (the 'father'/'mother' column) and 'unrelated people' (the 'father-in-law'/'mother-in-law' column) (Dunning, 1959, pp. 72-7, 109-19).

If you are wondering how an individual could possibly regard, say, his mother's brother as 'unrelated', then you are caught in an ethnocentric bind. But you may find some comfort in the fact that even the Ojibwa don't marry their 'relatives'. What is more worth noting, though, is that, so loaded with conjugal implications are the terms in my right-hand column, that, especially among some other Native Americans, anyone to whom any of these terms can be applied is a potential spouse (Basso, 1973, pp. 78-81, 88-90; Ridington, 1969; Shapiro, 1970a).

This Kariera:Ojibwa comparison can be pushed too far. Kariera, like most other Aboriginal terminologies, is consistently bifurcate, so that, for example, paternal and maternal grandparents are distinguished; whereas bifurcation in Ojibwa is limited to the medial three generations; and there are other differences in genealogical classification (Scheffler, 1971a). Perhaps more important for my interpretation is the fact that, generally in Aboriginal Australia, affinal relationships for a man are not confined to the wife's closest relatives; they include, for example, the wife's mother's brother—a member of the 'father' category—and would thus entail a violation of the kin/affine distinction.

They would, that is, in the absence of elaborations by which this distinction could be stressed. But, as it happens, these elaborations are nearly always made—though not, it seems, on a Kariera base, but on that of the first terminology we considered. This is so much the case that this terminology, as far as I know, nowhere exists in exactly the form given above, which is thus a simplification from more complex schemes. I think I can show that such a simplification is justifiable.

Probably the most common elaboration is the removal of

potential wife's mothers from the 'father's sister' category, which, as we shall see later, has profound implications. The thing to note now is that these two categories—'wife's mother' and 'father's sister'—are often separated only by subclassification.[5] In north-east Arnhem Land, for example, 'father's sister' is *mukul bapa*, 'wife's mother' *mukul rumaru*—that is the two are subcategories of the *mukul* category. The term *bapa* is the one for the 'father' category, while *rumaru* may be applied to any matrilineal kinsman of a potential wife; it has the connotations 'tabu' and 'to be avoided,' as such relatives should be.[6] Similarly, the ceremonial opposition 'mundane'/'sacred' (*yarangu/ duyu*) can be applied here: *mukul yarangu* = 'father's sister', *mukul duyu* = 'wife's mother'. Finally, individuals of both subcategories can be referred to simply as *mukul*. A 'wife's mother', however, cannot in this region be ritually transformed into a 'father's sister', as has been reported for other parts of the continent (Piddington, 1970, pp. 339-41; Thomson, 1972, p. 7).

Only superficially different considerations pertain to the reciprocal category 'man's child'. A Miwuyt woman and her brother call the latter's children *gatu*, and no man to whom she applies this term may be the woman's son-in-law. For this potential role the term *gurrung* is reserved. The two relationship terms do not seem to be linguistically similar; but several of my informants said they were 'the same', and under certain conditions could be used interchangeably. I conclude from this that *gatu* and *gurrung* are subcategories of a category which, unlike *mukul*, is unnamed.

There are other examples of subclassification in Miwuyt and other Aboriginal cultures which stress 'the importance of specifying . . . the status of desirable affines . . .' (Meggitt, 1962, p. 196); but the foregoing will suffice here. The most common elaboration of our first terminology is probably based on such subclassification. The classic example of this elaboration is the

---

[5] For his development of the notion of subclassification in Aboriginal relationship terminologies, I am again indebted to Harold Scheffler. See also Radcliffe-Brown (1951).
[6] Cf. Elkin (1940a, p. 333): '. . . usually, in Australian kinship, wife's mother is a father's sister "tabooed" . . .'.

relationship terminology of the Arunta (Aranda) of Central Australia (Spencer and Gillen, 1899, pp. 56-8, 74-7, 1927, pp. 43-61; see Map 1). A simpler and better analysed example, however, is provided by Hiatt's Gidjingali (Hiatt, 1965, pp. 38-47, 1968). The following is only a slightly simplified version of the Gidjingali pattern, arranged according to the Duwa/Yirritja moiety scheme which prevails in Arnhem Land:

own-moiety

'sibling'	'mother's mother'/'wife's mother's father'
'father'/'father's sister'	'wife's mother'/'wife's mother's brother'
'sibling'	'mother's mother'/'wife's mother's father'
'father'/'father's sister'	'wife's mother'/'wife's mother's brother'
'sibling'	'mother's mother'/'wife's mother's father'

opposite-moiety

'cousin'	'wife'/'wife's brother'
'mother'/'mother's brother'	'wife's father'
'cousin'	'wife'/'wife's brother'
'mother'/'mother's brother'	'wife's father'
'cousin'	'wife'/'wife's brother'

What has happened here, relative to our first terminology, is that each of the latter's categories have, as it were, split in two; for example, 'father' has become 'father' and 'wife's mother's brother', (male) 'cousin' has become (male) 'cousin' and 'wife's brother', etc. 'Mother' has become 'mother' and 'wife's father's sister', but this last category is unimportant and is not shown. Incidentally, everywhere in this representation where we encounter 'wife' or 'wife's . . .' we'd also find 'husband' or 'husband's . . .,' for the categories are the same regardless of Ego's sex. My choice of glosses is not so much a reflection of my own male bias as of the organization of Aboriginal life. As we shall see later, the mother-in-law and other senior affines who are so important in a man's career are much less significant in a woman's.

Note well that we have here not one but two sequences of patrifiliation in each moiety: I shall return to this point. Matrifiliation is also operative: indeed, it has been suggested that there are 'matrilineal' analogues to the Arunta/Gidjingali pattern (Ruhemann, 1945, pp. 544-6; Korn, 1973, ch. 4). And this pattern too sometimes exists in the absence of an exogamous dual division.

Appropriate spouse relationships in this terminology may be represented by the following list:

'sibling' and 'wife'/'wife's brother'
'father' and 'mother'
'father's sister' and 'mother's brother'
'mother's mother' and (male) 'cousin'
'wife's mother's father' and (female) 'cousin'
'wife's mother' and 'wife's father'

Here note that, within a patrifiliational sequence, the appropriate spouses of consecutive generations are located on *separate* patri-sequences of the opposite moiety. Thus, for example, the appropriate spouse of a 'father' is a 'mother', but that of a 'sibling' is not a 'cousin' but a 'wife' or a 'wife's brother'.

We can now return to the kin/affine distinction, which, I have intimated, is a salient one in Aboriginal thought. It might be well to recall that 'kin' implies no more than ineligibility for affinity and 'affine' no more than the potential of affinity. Even so, the elaborations effected by terminologies like Gidjingali are still too coarse to describe kin/affine distinctions in most of Aboriginal Australia. Consider the following:

First, in most Aboriginal cultures (though not Gidjingali), individuals of the 'mother's mother', 'wife's mother's father', 'wife's mother', and 'wife's mother's brother' categories who are members of the maternal grandmother's ritual lodge are ineligible as affines (Shapiro, 1971, p. 597).

Second, as we shall see, the wife's maternal grandmother and her siblings are important persons in the marital career of an Aboriginal man. Yet in the terminology under consideration they are lumped with sundry others in the 'cousin' category, many of whose members are not appropriate affines.

This leads to a third consideration. Although a 'cousin' is not an orthodox wife in most Aboriginal cultures, she is acceptable under certain contingencies. Such a marriage is not irregular or incestuous; it is a standardized alternative to the more proper union with a 'wife' (Piddington, 1970).

These and other ambiguities could readily be resolved by further subclassification; there is some evidence that this occurs in terminologies which still look very much like Gidjingali. Elsewhere, as in parts of the Kimberley Division of Western Australia (Map 1), this process seems to be giving rise to distinctive terminological schemes (Elkin, 1932b, pp. 312-15; Lucich, 1968).

You will recall that the Gidjingali terminology can be represented as four patri-sequences of terms. For many cultures there is evidence that, at least ideally, these are correlated with a four-part division of the ritual lodges relative to Ego. Ego accordingly applies the 'sibling'-'father' sequence to a quarter of the lodges of his tribe, including his own lodge; the 'cousin'-'mother' sequence to another quarter, including his mother's lodge; the 'wife'-'wife's father' sequence to a third quarter—the lodges of his actual and potential wives; and the 'mother's mother'-'wife's mother' sequence to the final quarter, including the lodge of his maternal grandmother, and those of his actual and potential mothers-in-law.

Now recall the dominance of matrifiliational rules in the use of relationship terms. Suppose a man I call 'father' is married to a woman I call 'mother'. No problem: whichever filiational path I choose, I shall have to call their children 'sibling'. But suppose this 'father' has another wife, whom I call not 'mother' but (say) 'cousin', as can and does happen. I could then apply 'sibling' to his children from this second wife too; but I am more likely to call them 'wife's mother' and 'wife's mother's brother', that is to invoke the matrifiliational rule for the children of a (female) 'cousin'. To this extent—and such studies as we have indicated that it is considerable—the neat pattern outlined in the preceeding paragraph is subverted.

But it is naive to regard this simply as a departure of 'reality' from 'ideals'. A more accurate view is that it is the result of the application of another set of 'ideals'—matrifiliational rules governing the assignment of relationship terms—which has priority over the first set. And that, in case you don't know by now, is another argument from principle![7]

Let us return now to Radcliffe-Brown's Kariera bromide which introduced this section—specifically, to the first two assertions I was able to tease out of it.

Are Aboriginal relationship terms really 'based on actual relations of consanguinity and affinity', and extended from these to relationships which are further removed genealogically— indeed, to relationships whose precise genealogical character is unknown to the Aborigines? Centering his argument on the Wikmunkan of the Cape York Peninsula (Map 1), the British anthropologist Rodney Needham (1962) has maintained that this is untenable. Thus to represent a native term as 'father', as I have done above, is acceptable as a convenience; but to believe that it signifies paternity, though applied to individuals who are not presumed to be one's father, is grossly ethnocentric. The meaning of the term, Needham holds, is to be found in what all the persons to whom it is appropriately applied have in common, and this is plainly not the relation of genitor to Ego. Every other relationship term is similarly assumed to have a single meaning which is equally applicable to all its referents—that is to be *monosemic*.

Needham's position has been devastated by Harold Scheffler (1972b, 1972c, 1973b, pp. 765-69) on both logical and empirical grounds. What has to concern us here is Scheffler's unearthing of linguistic data indicating that Aboriginal relationship terms in fact have several meanings—that they are *polysemic*, or rather (and I think this is stating the case more accurately), a single meaning which is *not* equally applicable to all referents. Which is to say that each of these terms signals a category which contains subcategories, one of which is primary

---

[7] It is also a·rudimentary form of what has been called a 'decision model'. For more elaborate examples of this very productive approach to ethnography, see Keesing (1967, 1970a). A less rigorous example is my analysis of Miwuyt residence groups (p. 23 *et seq.*).

or 'focal', the other(s) secondary or 'nonfocal'. The relationship between focal and nonfocal subcategories is said to be an extension of the former to the field covered by the latter. This extension is sometimes accomplished genealogically, if only in the limited sense of, for example, I call you 'sibling' because I called your father 'father' (cf. I call you 'sibling' because you are my father's brother's son) (Scheffler, 1972a). In other cases, however, the criteria are partly or wholly non-genealogical, though again the best examples are from outside Australia (e.g. Guemple, 1971; Kernan and Coult, 1965; Shapiro, 1970a).

I dealt earlier with another kind of subclassification in relationship terminologies, one in which both subcategories are equally focal. Thus in Miwuyt *mukul bapa* ('father's sister') and *mukul rumaru* ('wife's mother') are simply two kinds of *mukul*; neither is more or less *mukul* than the other. Now consider that the adjectives *dangang* ('full') and *marrkangga* ('partial') can be used to modify any relationship term in this language—say, *bapa* ('father'). It is *ipso facto* clear that a 'full father' is not only different from a 'partial father'; he is *more* of a 'father' as well. And this is precisely the sort of subclassification that most interests Scheffler.

Who, then, is a 'full father'? When I first heard these adjectives used to modify relationship terms, I assumed that a 'full' member of any category is simply the occupant of that category who is genealogically closest to Ego. This assumption, I think, stemmed from a general ethnocentrism, as well as from a rarer parochialism that pervades the culture of kinship buffs.[8] Thus I was certain that a 'full father' is none other than one's real, true, genuine and (above all) socially presumed father.

But I was wrong. The Miwuyt subcategory 'full father' does indeed include one's genitor, but it embraces others as well—specifically, any 'father' who is a member of one's genitor's (and one's own) ritual lodge. All other 'fathers' are 'partial fathers'. Analogous notions apply to the subclassification of other Miwuyt relationship categories.

---

[8] As Hocart (1937) saw, this parochialism derives from the use of genealogies alone in eliciting relationship terminologies. See also Schneider (1972).

This is not to say that Miwuyt lacks a term which really is equivalent to our 'father': I have already mentioned that it has such a term—'finder' (chapter 1). But this word (*malkmara-namirri*) is clearly unrelated linguistically to 'father' (*bapa*); and, although a 'finder' is a special kind of 'father', he is not more of a 'father' than is, say, a father's brother.

Thus, although Miwuyt relationship terms are polysemic and entail a focal/nonfocal distinction, this is not of the sort Radcliffe-Brown seems to have had in mind or that Scheffler generally espouses. There is some indication that this is broadly true of Aboriginal relationship terminologies, and that other anthropologists have been misled by their own special ethno-centrism (see p. 57 n. 8 and Shapiro, 1969c, 1971).

These considerations lead rather directly to the second asser-tion derived from Radcliffe-Brown—that in Aboriginal societies, everybody is a kinsman to everybody else. We could perhaps now argue that this is so, though not to the same degree: thus a 'full father' is a 'closer' relative than a 'partial father', etc. This was Radcliffe-Brown's position, and there are innumerable state-ments to this effect in the ethnographic literature.

But I suspect this is a mistaken notion. There is considerable evidence that Aboriginal cultures have concepts which are reasonably similar to the ones we label with such terms as 'kin' (as opposed to 'nonkin') and 'relatives' (as opposed to 'unrelated people')—that is concepts which some anthropologists like to call 'kindreds' (Mitchell, 1963; Scheffler, 1973b, p. 751). Terms which can be translated as 'kindred' exist in Miwuyt and have been reported for other Aboriginal languages (Berndt and Berndt, 1970, p. 76; Elkin, 1938a, p. 436; McKnight, 1971, p. 148; Stanner, 1933a, pp. 395-6; Thomson, 1972, pp. 3, 18). Similarly, my informants often made comments of the form, 'A and B are in the X:Y relationship, but not really—only by relationship term', that is the two individuals named are not members of each other's kindreds.

Assuming, then, that kindreds are general in Aboriginal Australia, I believe that whether these social units are exogamous or endogamous will turn out to be a salient distinction in Aboriginal ethnography. Meggitt's Walbiri analysis (1962), for example, strongly suggests the presence of exogamous kindreds in Central Australia, whereas endogamous kindreds are certain for north-east Arnhem Land. Outside of these and a few other cases, however, our data on this score are grossly deficient: we need to know more about subclassification in Aboriginal relationship terminologies; about native concepts of the kindred order; and about the idiomization of affinal norms in these terms.

SEVEN

Four- and eight-class systems

In chapter 5 we examined one general kind of social unit whose numerical aspect, unlike that of ritual lodges and matrilineal groups, is vital. Here I want to have a look at other arrangements of this sort, but whose membership is greater than two. In Aboriginal Australia such schemes have either four or eight members.

The four-member systems, at least, were known in Morgan's day, and they played an important role in his conjectures about human social evolution (Morgan, 1877, 1880; Fison and Howitt, 1880). But it was Radcliffe-Brown's study of Kariera culture that provided the basis for modern discussion of these schemes:

> The Kariera tribe is divided into four parts that I shall speak of as *classes*. The names of these are Banaka, Burung, Palyeri, and Karimera. . . . These classes regulate the marriages of the natives. A man of any given class is restricted in his choice of a wife to one of the other classes. Thus a Banaka man may only marry a Burung woman and a Burung man may only marry a Banaka woman. The two classes, Banaka and Burung, thus form what will be spoken of as an *intermarrying pair* or simply a *pair*. This does not imply that a Banaka man may marry *any* Burung woman, but only that he may not marry a woman of any other class. The child of a Banaka man and a Burung woman is neither Banaka nor Burung but Palyeri, while the child of a Burung man and a Banaka woman is Karimera (Radcliffe-Brown, 1913, pp. 147-8).

Such rules were succinctly represented by Radcliffe-Brown (ibid., p. 148) as follows:

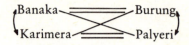

With which came this explication:

> The sign ═══════ connects the two classes of an intermarrying pair and therefore shows the relation of husband and wife. The sign ⌡ connects the class of a mother with the class of her child. I propose to speak of the classes so related as together forming a *cycle*. . . . Banaka and Karimera form one cycle and Burung and Palyeri the other. The children of a woman always belong to the same cycle as herself but to the other class of the cycle. The sign ╱ connects the class of a father with the class of his child. I propose to speak of the two classes so connected as together forming a *couple*. . . . Banaka and Palyeri form one couple and Karimera and Burung form the other. The children of a man always belong to the same couple as himself, but to the other class of the couple (ibid., p. 148).[1]

Note that the two 'couples' are structurally equivalent to a patri-moiety system; such as division, we saw in the preceding chapter, is expressly recognized in Kariera culture. Similarly, the two 'cycles' are equivalent to a matri-moiety scheme and the two 'pairs' to a set of 'generation' moieties, though arrangements like these may not be codified in Kariera (but see pp. 72-4). Faced with facts of this sort, some anthropologists speak of 'implicit moieties'; but this really adds nothing to the ethnography, since it is the anthropologists, not the Aborigines, to whom the moieties are implicit (Dumont, 1966). Still, such notions do have the heuristic value of pointing to possible gaps in the data.

For Aboriginal social units are sometimes distinguished by more subtle criteria than those recognized by certain writers (see esp. Goody, 1961). The Karadjeri of the Kimberley Division of Western Australia (Map 1), who have a four-class system

---

[1] Although this does not diminish the value of Radcliffe-Brown's exposition, it should be noted that many of the terms, concepts, and classificatory schemes he utilized were invented or discovered not by him but by the Victorian anthropologist R. H. Mathews. See Elkin (1956), which includes a bibliography of Mathews's work.

identical in structure and nearly identical in nomenclature to that of the Kariera, provide several illustrations:

> The Karadjeri . . . [classes] are grouped in various ways, though there are no proper names for the [resultant] moieties. Thus the patrilineal moieties (Burung-Karimba and Panaka-Paljeri) have no special names, but each man calls his own moiety *nganirangu* and the other *kalyera*. Each of the two intermarrying pairs of . . . [classes] (Panaka-Burung and Karimba-Paljeri) is called *mreramrera, umalanguru* or *inara*, one being termed Panaburung and the other Karimpaljeringuru [i.e. compounds of the names of the classes of the pair]. A matrilineal moiety (Panaka-Karimba or Burung-Paljeri) is called *kagaramada* or *kagarangu* . . . (Piddington, 1970, p. 330).

Karadjeri culture, then contains three kinds of moiety division, and these are formally identical to those of the Walbiri (chapter 5). Such a situation is probably far more common in Aboriginal Australia than the ethnographic literature would lead one to believe.

The arrangement of classes within each Kariera (or Karadjeri) patri-moiety, such that, for example, the son of a Banaka man is Palyeri and the son of that man Banaka again, recalls the 'merging of alternative generations' pattern of most Aboriginal relationship terminologies. In fact, the four-class system is precisely congruent with the first terminology we considered in the preceding chapter. Given Ego's class, every relationship term is located in a particular class: thus if I am Banaka, other Banaka people are in the 'sibling' category with respect to me; Burung people are my 'cousins', Karimera people my 'mothers' and 'mother's brothers', Palyeri people my 'fathers' and 'father's sisters'.

The system is not, however, as Radcliffe-Brown and others have thought, congruent with the Kariera relationship terminology—for exactly the same reasons that an exogamous moiety scheme is not (pp. 48-50). But the assumption of such congruence allowed Radcliffe-Brown to assert that 'the classes regulate the marriage of the natives'. This was more genuinely the position of the nineteenth century anthropologists, who dubbed these divisions 'marriage classes' or 'matrimonial classes'. One of Radcliffe-Brown's first pontifical acts was to exorcise the diabolical modifers 'marriage' and 'matrimonial' from these labels. The justification for this started with the following argument:

> It was stated earlier that a man of the Banaka class can only marry a woman of the Burung class. We are now able to explain what this rule means. In the Kariera tribe a man may only marry a woman who stands to him in the relation of ['cousin']. If the man is Banaka his ['cousin'] is Burung, and therefore in saying that he must marry a ['cousin'], we are saying that he must marry a Burung woman (Radcliffe-Brown, 1913, p. 155).

By this argument, then, the class system and the relationship terminology are different but effectively equivalent codes for the idiomization of marital norms. But not *quite* equivalent, for, as Radcliffe-Brown realized, in the Burung class are certain women whom a Banaka man may *not* marry—for example, his paternal grandmother and his daughter's daughter, who are not (or at least not unless the notion of subclassification is invoked) in the 'cousin' relationship category. From this Radcliffe-Brown reached the following conclusion:

> The marriage rule of the Kariera is simplicity itself: a man may marry a woman who is his ['cousin'], but he may marry no one else. Thus we may say that in the Kariera tribe marriage is regulated by relationship and by relationship alone (ibid.).

'Relationship' here clearly means 'relationship terminology', as opposed to the class system: hence the purging of 'marriage' from 'marriage class'. Soon (Radcliffe-Brown, 1918) 'class' was no longer acceptable either, since, as Radcliffe-Brown later remarked, 'In sociology it is convenient to reserve the term "class" . . . for social groups marked off from one another by differences of rank or occupation' (1931, p. 6). Thus was born the vogue of referring to the Kariera divisions as 'sections', still very much the rage even in this late season.

Although Australian Aboriginal anthropology does not quite stand or fall on this issue, I propose resurrecting the term 'class' in the form Radcliffe-Brown originally used it. After all, at a time when 1940-ish modes are again dominating the fashion scene, would it not be more chic still to return to the styles of 1913?—all the more so when the schemes thus labelled, as we shall see, seem themselves often to be creatures of whimsy! There is also the consideration that by using 'sections', I shall help you confuse the divisions of 'the Kariera tribe' with the divisions of this book. Then too, while 'class' may suggest 'socioeconomic class', my teaching experience has been that students take 'sections' to mean 'section of town' or somesuch. Finally, as Lévi-Strauss (1966) has reminded us, classification is a fundamental property of human thought, not only in ivory towers but in city streets and on jungle paths and desert tracks too. We shall see that Aboriginal *class systems* are just this sort of thing—native logical schemes. Let the sociologists find another term!

So much for the mechanics of the *four-class* systems. The divisions in *eight-class* systems, as Radcliffe-Brown (1910) initially called them, he later (1918) termed 'subsections'—a convention that has survived to the present. Again I move to return to the original nomenclature, and for the same reasons plus one additional: although from a continent-wide standpoint, the eight-class schemes, as we shall see, entail a subdivision of the four, any single tribe (if it has such classes at all) has either four or eight—not both, as the term 'subsection' suggests.

The classic example of an eight-class system is that of the Arunta. Happily, this is also the best-documented example, having been studied first-hand by Spencer and Gillen (1899, pp. 70-3, 1927, pp. 41-5), Porteus (1931, pp. 133-4), Pink (1936), Strehlow (1947, 1965, pp. 134-9), Roheim (1950, pp. 47-54) and others.[2] Radcliffe-Brown's summary representation of the system (1931, p. 8) is something of an eyesore, and more than something of a mind-boggler, so we had best bypass it. Here, at least, one word may be worth a thousand pictures.[3]

---

[2] I list here only those sources which are in English and which can be found in most substantial libraries. Other sources, including some recent second-hand analyses, are in German, while still others, though in English, are lodged in journals with only a limited circulation.

[3] The diagramming of Aboriginal class systems has become a minor anthropological tradition in its own right. Perhaps the most analytically useful scheme (and certainly the

Recall that in the Kariera class system there are two 'pairs' and two 'couples'. The fundamental difference between this and the Arunta scheme is that the latter contains *four* pairs and *four* couples. Within each couple, in both Kariera and Arunta, there is the by now familiar merging of alternate generations, such that a man, his father's father, and his son's son are in one class of the couple, his father and son in the other class. The Arunta classes, like the Kariera, can be arranged into two matrilineal 'cycles': each Arunta cycle thus contains four classes, as compared with only two in its Kariera counterpart.

There is otherwise no indication of a matri-moiety division. A *patri*-moiety scheme, however, is explicit in Arunta culture, and each patri-moiety contains four classes. Further, the arrangement of the eight classes into four couples is expressly recognized by the Arunta. Hence two couples are associated with each moiety. If we take four father-son sequences of five generations each to illustrate the merging of alternate generations within a couple, the articulation of patri-moieties, couples, and classes in Arunta may be represented as follows:

Moiety X: Couple P: 1	Couple Q: 3
2	4
1	3
2	4
1	3

Moiety Y: Couple R: 5	Couple S: 7
6	8
5	7
6	8
5	7

The numbers 1-8 represent the classes. I use this notation in preference to the Arunta terms mainly for simplicity's sake, but also because the latter are somewhat differently rendered into English script by different anthropologists. The use of P, Q, R,

clearest) is that of Hammel (1960, 1966, p. 4), which also deals with cases, many of them hypothetical, other than the two considered here. See also Barnes (1967, pp. 9-22).

and S for the couples follows the convention established by Radcliffe-Brown (1931, p. 9), who called such divisions *semi-moieties* (chapter 8).

The Arunta pairs are as follows:

> 1 and 7
> 2 and 6
> 3 and 5
> 4 and 8

Note that the appropriate 'spouse' classes of the two classes of any couple are located in different couples of the opposite moiety. In more familiar terms, an Arunta man is supposed to take a wife not only of a different class from the one his father did (as in Kariera), but of a different couple altogether: his wife should not be a member of his mother's class or even of her couple. This is strikingly reminiscent of the rule in the Gidjingali relationship terminology (pp. 52-3) that the appropriate spouse of a (male) 'sibling' is not a (female) 'cousin', that is the daughter of a 'mother's brother', but a 'wife'. In fact, the Gidjingali have a class system identical to that of the Arunta (Hiatt, 1965, pp. 47-50, 1968, pp. 173-4), and both systems are precisely congruent with the Gidjingali relationship terminology. Thus, for example, if I am a member of class 1, my co-members are my 'siblings'; members of class 2 are my 'fathers' and 'father's sisters'; of class 3, my 'mother's mothers' and 'wife's mother's fathers'; of class 4, my 'wife's mothers' and 'wife's mother's brothers'; of class 5, my 'cousins'; of class 6, my 'mothers' and 'mother's brothers'; of class 7, my 'wives' and 'wife's brothers'; of class 8, my 'wife's fathers' (and their sisters).

As might be expected, actual marriages in societies with either four- or eight-class systems sometimes violate the notion of appropriate pairs. An Arunta man of class 1, for example, though he should marry a woman of class 7, may instead take a wife of class 5. To which class, in this case, would the children of the marriage be assigned? To class 2, on the basis of patrifiliation, or to class 4, through matrifiliation? Elkin's reply in favour of the priority of the latter rule—that the father is 'thrown away' (presumably a translation of a native expression)—has come to be taken as anthropological gospel, and seems indeed to hold for the majority of Aboriginal tribes (Elkin, 1964, pp. 103-4, 108-9). But certainly not for all. The Arunta are the most famous advocates of 'throwing the *mother* away' when it comes to class assignment of the child (Radcliffe-Brown, 1910; Pink, 1936, pp. 297-8; Strehlow, 1947, pp. 127-8; Korn, 1973, pp. 28-9; cf. Elkin, 1933a, p. 68), and there are other examples, among both four- and eight-class tribes (Falkenberg, 1962, pp. 226-7; Fry, 1934, p. 473; Piddington, 1970, pp. 332-4; Reay, 1962; Wilson, 1970, p. 339).

Where matrifiliation does take precedence in class assignment, alternate or improper marriages interfere with the realization of ideals concerning couples. Thus in the hypothetical case just noted, the children of the man of class 1 would, under matrifiliation, be members of class 4. And this could snowball: if such a class 4 son married properly, that is a woman of class 8, his own son would be class 3. Et cetera. In order to right things as quickly as possible, the class 4 son would have to be a party to an unorthodox match—that is with a class 6 woman, whose children would *ipso facto* be class 1, the unit of their paternal grandfather.

The frequency with which such departures could take place is often limited by an insistence on patri-moiety exogamy. Thus a man of class 1, whose orthodox wife is of class 7, could get away with marriages to women of classes 5, 6, and 8 as well; yet he could under no circumstances have a wife of classes 1-4. But where moieties are not strictly exogamous or are absent altogether, the sky (if anyone wanted to marry it) might well be the limit. In any case, short of taking the pairs with complete seriousness—something few if any tribes do—the only way to guarantee complete realization of the couples is to do as the Arunta do: embrace the principle of patrifiliation in class assignment.

Regardless of whether patri- or matrifiliation is given priority, Aboriginal class systems provide the best documented examples of the principle of social classification we first encountered in the Duwa/Yirritja division. We can now generalize this principle:

*In a system of social units in which an individual's position is
determined by kinship criteria, his location is not that of the
determining kinsman.*

The word 'not' is crucial here; if it is omitted, we have the
principle of recruitment to ritual lodges, matrilineal groups, and
many other kinds of social unit (Shapiro, 1967a).

In the preceding chapter I noted that in cultures with relationship terminologies similar to Arunta and Gidjingali, 'cousin'
is, under certain circumstances, an acceptable if less than
orthodox spouse category. This alternative is coded into most
eight-class systems by a sort of second level of pairs, which can
be represented as follows:

> 1 and 5
> 2 and 8
> 3 and 7
> 4 and 6

It seems a bit strange that, if the class systems are as epi-
phenomenal to marriage as Radcliffe-Brown believed, the first
Australians should bother with this alternate set of pairings.
There is also the consideration that, between Aborigines not
sufficiently acquainted with each other to be able to apply the
principles of patri- and matrifiliation in the relationship terminology, class labels are used to determine appropriate relationship terms (Service, 1960): for example, a man of class 1 who
meets for the first time a certain other man need only know that
the latter is a member of, say, class 4 to call him 'wife's mother's
brother', and to regard his sister as a potential mother-in-law.
Where kindreds are exogamous (pp. 57-8), this may be sufficient to initiate an affinal relationship. In some situations, in
short, it may well be that, although the relationship terminology
provides an idiom for marital norms, the application of this
idiom depends on the class system.

Admittedly, this turning around of the Radcliffe-Brown position is conjecture (but see Fry, 1933; Elkin, 1940b; Yengoyan,
1970, p. 86). Yet there are more concrete indications that, in
some areas, classes are marriage classes after all. The coastal
Miwuyt are good textbook Aborigines, more or less ignoring

their eight-class system in the politics of marriage, and 'throwing away' the father in the class assignment of children. But their fellow tribesmen further inland (with whom they rarely marry) have never read Radcliffe-Brown or Elkin. They take the affinal norms of the class system unusually seriously, and when an incorrect marriage occurs they 'correct' not only the wife's class membership but that of her matrikin as well (cf. Elkin, 1950, p. 11). Word of their earnestness has reached the maritimers, at least some of whom wonder if they too should not join the fold. By the time I left north-east Arnhem Land in 1967 there were indications that even the coastal Miwuyt were genuinely using the class system in marriage, if only to justify (or discredit) particular unions (see also Berndt, 1962, pp. 73-4, 1965, p. 82).

The case of the Murinbata of south-west Arnhem Land (Map 2) is broadly similar, and it raises more salient issues. For its elucidation, we are indebted to two rich ethnographic studies separated by a decade and a half—the first by the Australian anthropologist W. E. H. Stanner in 1935, followed by his Norwegian colleague Johannes Falkenberg in 1950. Writing in 1936, Stanner (1936a, p. 209) notes that among the Murinbata the eight-class system 'commenced to spread at the most not more than one generation ago'. 'Few of the women know with certainty what their . . . [classes] are, and fewer children do. Many of the men are equally vague' (p. 210).

> One or two . . . natives are regarded . . . as experts in the new fashions. Each of them is a traveller, having roamed beyond the tribal homelands . . . They have been schooled in alien camps until they know perfectly . . . how the . . . [classes] work (p. 208).

The notion that the eight-class system constitutes a new fashion among the Murinbata is worth pursuing:

> The Murinbata have been under a certain compulsion to accept the . . . [eight-class] system. Tribes peripheral to the . . . [eight-class] area seem to feel an inferiority at not possessing, nor understanding, . . . [the eight-class system]. The belief that they are marrying . . . wrongly has been implanted in them, associated with the feeling that the . . . [eight-class] organization . . . [and other forms of social organization] which are being diffused at the

same time, are in some way superior to those they possess historically (p. 186).

With characteristic sensitivity, Stanner presents the plight of a man who had been imprisoned by Europeans before the eight-class rage caught on among the Murinbata:

> Returning to his tribe after many years in gaol, old Kambut is one among many who has not caught up with the new jargon. He sees the same camps, the same faces, the same outward swing of nomad life, but sees also a new and bewildering criss-cross segmentation of his tribe which eludes his understanding. There is little about it that is even tangible. The camps are not being split up into eight physical divisions in one of which, knowing where he was, he could live out what is left of his life. The camps are as before. Instead, every person in the tribe, himself among them, bears a new and scarcely understood label which seriously limits the freedom once possessed. . . . Particularly baffling to such a person are the marriage rules of the new order, but the younger men are ready with ridicule for hesitancy and conservatism. The new fashions seem to be irresistible, so great is their momentum. They are known to have come a long way, from . . . land which no Murinbata had ever seen . . . (p. 202).

Even if you do not share old Kambut's bewilderment at the eight-class system, its creeping stylishness among his people surely strikes familiar notes. At any rate, Stanner's perceptive analysis was later generalized at a distance by A. L. Kroeber, who referred to such classificatory schemes as 'the play of earnest children, or the inventive vagaries of fashion' (1952, p. 224). Further, they

> . . . would thus represent a field of experimentation or play . . ., a fact that accords with their intricacy and variety . . . They would be among the more variable and unstable constituents of culture—among its fashions . . . This would not in the least imply that they were regarded as trivial. In fact highly impermanent fashions of dress, etiquette, conduct, and belief may be held to with emotional intensity, and the insistence on conformity to them may be very powerful . . . p. 217).

That class systems are as ephemeral as Kroeber suggested is

open to substantial doubt: in many parts of Australia they are articulated with the scheme of lodge-estates, and there are myths accounting for their origin (e.g. Berndt, 1970b; Elkin, 1940a, pp. 326-7; Kaberry, 1937; Strehlow, 1947, pp. 127-30, 139-50). Still, his assimilation of them to the world of fashion is not only quintessentially appropriate to the Murinbata case; it also gives us further insight into the wider intertribal spread of such schemes.

All this is a worthwhile digression, but a digression nonetheless. Let us return to 'the marriage rules of the new order' among the Murinbata. Stanner (1936a, p. 198) notes that the eight classes 'are spreading specifically as marriage groupings'. This by itself calls into question the Radcliffe-Brown position. But perhaps even more devastating is Stanner's observation that, apparently as a result of the introduction of the eight-class system, the Murinbata relationship terminology has begun to be altered. The details of these changes need not trouble us here; I should note, though, that they signal an incipient Gidjingali-like system emerging from something similar to the first terminology considered in the preceding chapter (ibid., pp. 197-200).

Falkenberg's re-study of the Murinbata supports Stanner's analysis and shows that, by 1950, the influence of the intrusive eight-class system had become even more profound. Thus the relationship terminology had moved still closer to the Gidjingali model; and individual relationships were frequently changed so as to jibe with the class affiliations of the individuals concerned (Falkenberg, 1962, pp. 213-25, 232-6). Particularly noteworthy is Falkenberg's eliciting of native statements to the effect that, before the introduction of the classes,

> . . . it was sometimes difficult to work out the correct relationship between individuals. . . . primarily, the Murinbata consider the [eight-class] system . . . as a useful guide to marriage. . . . there were formerly a considerable number of irregular marriages . . ., and according to the Aborigines, the system of . . . [classes] aids them in determining correct marriage mates (p. 232).

Other examples of the use of class systems in marital decisions can be found in Elkin (1940a, pp. 308-26), Gould (1969, pp. 174-6), Kaberry (1937), Pink (1936, pp. 297-9), Reay (1962), Stanner (1933a, pp. 398-400), Strehlow (1947), and Wilson (1970, pp. 338-9). See also the comments by Lévi-Strauss in Lee and DeVore (1968, p. 213).

Radcliffe-Brown's *ex cathedra* rejection of such cases seems to have been grounded in certain considerations most clearly spelled out in his last general review of social organization in Aboriginal Australia. Note the re-appearance of the anathematized term 'class'—with its sacrilegious influence presumably contained by quotation marks:

> (1) . . . in Australian tribes the arrangement of marriages is carried out by reference to [relationship terminologies] . . . (2) . . . tribes with the same 'class' system, for example with four 'classes', have different marriage systems [as defined by their relationship terminologies], while the same marriage system can be found in tribes having different 'class' systems. This thesis . . . has been confirmed by field studies in many part of Australia by various other anthropological investigators (Radcliffe-Brown, 1951, p. 38).

Proposition (2) is undeniable, and must be counted as one of Radcliffe-Brown's most important discoveries in the Aboriginal field. But Proposition (1) by no means follows, though Radcliffe-Brown apparently assumed it did. This circularity could then be defended on the grounds, themselves true, that Proposition (1) 'has been confirmed by field studies in many parts of Australia . . .'. What Radcliffe-Brown completely ignored were those studies that indicated otherwise.

It has to be mentioned here, as if in left-handed veneration of Radcliffe-Brown, that neither the four- nor the eight-class system is ever a *sufficient* determinant of appropriate spouse relationships. Thus under the latter, as under the former, a man's paternal grandmother and his daughter's daughter are in the 'spouse' class, but no Aboriginal tribe permits marriage with these relatives. More, most cultures with eight-class systems even further restrict a man's conjugal sphere—as when a woman of the proper class may not be married if her mother is a lodgemate of one's maternal grandmother.

Such rules would appear to entail a drastic limitation on the choice of mates. This effect, however, is at least partly countered by certain alternate marriage possibilities, the most common of which has already been noted (see also Piddington, 1970), and by the frequent if not usual existence of eight-class systems in the numerically largest tribes (Yengoyan, 1968; cf. Meggitt, 1968).

The Murinbata case detailed above, far from being exceptional, is only the best documented example of the spread and integration of a class system into a new setting. There is in fact a substantial literature on the communication of such systems at traditional intertribal gatherings and their modern counterparts, mission and government settlements; the temporary incorporation of both Aboriginal and European visitors into local categorical schemes; and the remarkable ingenuity of the first Australians in adjusting one class system to another and to other forms of social classification (Berndt and Berndt, 1964, pp. 48-53; Elkin, 1931b, p. 72, 1932b, pp. 323-6, 1933a, p. 68, 1939, pp. 198-201, 1940a, pp. 308-32, 1940b, 1950, pp. 3-16, 1963, pp. 99-107, 1964, pp. 103-8; Fry, 1933, p. 267; Gould, 1969, pp. 108, 174-8; Kaberry, 1937; Kelly, 1935, pp. 463-4; Long, 1970a, p. 324; Reay, 1962, 1970; Spencer, 1914, pp. 60-4; Spencer and Gillen, 1899, pp. 68-9, 1904, pp. 117-23, 1927, p. 43; Stanner, 1933a, pp. 397-402, 1933c; Strehlow, 1965, p. 130; Warner, 1933, pp. 76-8, 1937, pp. 116-23; Wilson, 1970, p. 338; Yengoyan, 1970, pp. 86-7—and this is only a partial enumeration!).

So far I have discussed Aboriginal class systems primarily from a 'social use' standpoint. I want to turn now to their more cognitive aspects. These latter, though known casually to anthropology for some time, have received special attention recently by C. G. von Brandenstein of the University of Western Australia.

Von Brandenstein (1970) is concerned to show that four-class systems in many parts of Australia are schemes for the classification of natural forms, as well as of human anatomical and psychological traits. We encountered this sort of thing in exogamous moiety systems. In four-class arrangements, however, the classificatory principles seem much less arbitrary, both in themselves and in their articulation with the cycles and pairs. Thus the relationship between the two pairs seems to be widely conceptualized by such oppositions as cold/hot and cold-blooded/warm-blooded, particularly as applied to animals and other natural forms (classified here, as in moiety schemes, generically). Meanwhile, the conceptual relationship between the cycles seems best summarized by the opposition active/passive, applied to both human beings (as in moiety schemes, specifically categorized) and natural forms. With respect to the Kariera classes, these notions yield the following:

	active	passive
cold	Banaka	Burung
hot	Karimera	Palyeri

Thus all species of lizard, being cold-blooded, are in the Banaka-Burung pair; but a variety known colloquially as 'savage goanna', that is an active form, is more precisely Banaka, whereas the 'lazy goanna', as a passive form, is Burung. Similarly, all kinds of kangaroo, as warm-blooded creatures, are in the Karimera-Palyeri pair; the aggressive plains kangaroo is Karimera, while its more subdued cousin, the hill kangaroo, is Palyeri. Fire, something active and hot, is Karimera; dew, because of its coldness and passivity, is Burung.

In the human domain, individuals of the Banaka-Karimera (active) cycle are supposed to be hot-headed, fast, industrious, and of wiry physique; those of the Burung-Palyeri (passive) cycle to be gentle, slow, lazy, and fat. That in real life some Banaka-Karimera people display some or all Burung-Palyeri traits and vice versa is apparently of no concern to the Aborigines: what we are dealing with here is a cultural dogma, not a set of observed statistical regularities (cf. Valentine, 1963).

This ideology, moreover, may be part of another we have already encountered. Von Brandenstein has so far—his research is still in progress—been unable to discover substantial differences between the two classes *within* a cycle as regards supposedly associated traits. I suggest this is not an accident, and that no such differences exist. This would be consistent with the notion that matrilineally-related individuals share the same mundane attributes (chapter 4).[4] More, it would indicate a matri-moiety division in Kariera and other four-class systems which could not be dismissed as 'implicit' (p. 60).

Some of the alleged correlations among these traits, for example, that between fatness and laziness, seem to fit European stereotypes. The idea that bodily and temperamental differences are parentally-determined also hits home—though Aborigines seem to depart from our folk notions in their stress on the maternal origin or individual variation (but see p. 74, note 4). Familiar too is the incorporation into a single frame of reference of human and animal attributes: we speak of certain people as being 'rat-faced' or 'as clever as a fox', and we have public fantasies in which animals with such specific/generic labels as Mickey Mouse and Donald Duck form a single society. An earlier generation of anthropologists considered this sort of thing to be childish prattle, but it is *their* assumptions that have since been shown to be immature (Hallowell, 1955, ch. 2). Recent suggestive analyses inspired by Lévi-Strauss (1966) signal a new appreciation of such areas of human thought (Berndt, 1970b; Leach, 1964).

Von Brandenstein's work points the way to the cracking of a code for the organization of human experience that spans the entire Australian continent. In this respect it is comparable to the set of related dichotomies adduced in chapter 4, and to Radcliffe-Brown's analysis of Aboriginal moiety schemes (chapter 5).

[4] Individuation in the sacred sphere is most often effected by schemes of personal names. These are articulated with ritual lodge ideology in a manner which conforms broadly to the pattern sketched by Lévi-Strauss (1966, pp. 151-3). It is worth adding that personal names in Aboriginal Australia are indeed personal: individuals, especially adult males, should be addressed not by name but by relationship term or class.

EIGHT

Semi-moiety organization

Recall the Arunta couples which, following Radcliffe-Brown (1931, p. 9), I dubbed P, Q, R, and S. Radcliffe-Brown saw fit to call each of these a 'semi-moiety', since each couple is equivalent to half a (patri-)moiety.[1] But he had a broader view of *semi-moiety organization*. Thus the Mara of the south-western shores of the Gulf of Carpentaria (Map 1) have a patri-moiety system but no classes. Instead, each moiety is split into two named and apparently patrilineal divisions—each of which is known by the Mara to be congruent with one of the couples in the eight-class systems of adjacent tribes (Spencer, 1914, pp. 60-4; Spencer and Gillen, 1904, pp. 116-30). This congruence was for Radcliffe-Brown sufficient grounds to call the Mara divisions 'semi-moieties' too (Radcliffe-Brown, 1931, pp. 8-10).

Elkin (1964, pp. 111-13), however, has departed from this catholic position: for him, semi-moieties are couples in an eight-class system and that's that. A clue to the justification for this heresy is perhaps provided in a more recent study of Mara social organization by Marie Reay of The Australian National University. Following Elkin's lead, Reay (1962, p. 99) suggests that we discard the label 'semi-moieties' for the divisions of the Mara and neighbouring tribes and, in accordance with more

---

[1] In a four-class system each class is also equivalent to half a patri-moiety, but it ideally links patrilineal kinsmen only in alternate generations. Semi-moieties have more room: a man belongs, again ideally, to the same semi-moiety as his father's father and son's son, *and* his father and son. They thus look like true patrilineal units, but as we shall see they often are not. For now, forget about four-class systems: semi-moiety organization can be articulated only with eight-class schemes.

general anthropological usage, call them 'patrilineal descent groups, which they are'.

But are they really? Let us return to the pioneer study of Mara social organization by Spencer and Gillen (1904, pp. 116-30). These authors give the two moiety names as Urku and Ua, the former composed of the divisions Murungun and Mumbali, the latter Purdal and Kuial. And they note, in each case referring to males as parents, that 'the children of Murungun are Murungun; of Purdal, Purdal; of Mumbali, Mumbali; of Kuial, Kuial' (p. 119). This seems simple enough.

But Spencer and Gillen (pp. 119-20) further note that each of these four divisions 'really consists' of two subdivisions, 'which, for the sake of clearness', they designate by the Greek letters *alpha* and *beta*. Within each division, the son of an *alpha* man is ideally *beta* and vice versa. The ideal pattern over five generations is thus:

Urku moiety:	Murungun *alpha*	Mumbali *alpha*
	Murungun *beta*	Mumbali *beta*
	Murungun *alpha*	Mumbali *alpha*
	Murungun *beta*	Mumbali *beta*
	Murungun *alpha*	Mumbali *alpha*
Ua moiety:	Purdal *alpha*	Kuial *alpha*
	Purdal *beta*	Kuial *beta*
	Purdal *alpha*	Kuial *alpha*
	Purdal *beta*	Kuial *beta*
	Purdal *alpha*	Kuial *alpha*

This by now should be somewhere between familiar and tiresome. It is the old Arunta/Gidjingali relationship terminology/eight-class pattern with only a superficially new twist. Even the orthodox marriages are analogous:

> Murungun *alpha* and Purdal *alpha*
> Murungun *beta* and Kuial *beta*
> Mumbali *alpha* and Kuial *alpha*
> Mumbali *beta* and Purdal *beta*

Since the Mara presumably have yet to learn Greek, one might want to know how a member of that tribe knows that he or she or anybody is (say) Murungun *alpha* as opposed to Murungun *beta*. Elsewhere, Spencer (1914, p. 60) tells us that the subdivisions have no names in the Mara language: hence one possibility can be immediately dismissed. In fact, neither Spencer nor Gillen seems to have realized the appropriateness of the question, let alone supplied an answer. But Reay's later study provides a clue:

> The clear distinction between alternate generations in the . . .
> [eight-class] system is absent from the system of semi-moieties. A
> man's wife has to belong to the same moiety as his mother, but a
> different semi-moiety. There is no simple means of establishing
> which semi-moiety his wife must come from apart from reference
> to the semi-moiety of his mother. (Reay, 1962, p. 96).

This is reminiscent of the eight-class notion that a man's wife should not be a member of his mother's couple. More to the point, though, is the suggestion that an individual's position within a semi-moiety, which Spencer and Gillen mark by *alpha* and *beta*, is determined by the semi-moiety of his mother— though mother and child belong to different divisions. This in turn is still another exemplification of the principle we first encountered in the Duwa/Yirritja scheme and which I generalized in the preceding chapter. No one except the Mara themselves may know just how they idiomize such positioning, but this is a secondary consideration. My own guess, for what it is worth, is that this is done in a fashion similar to the way the Miwuyt express the relationship between an individual and his mother's ritual lodge (chapter 4). I would thus expect to find in the Mara language forms like 'Murungun, Kuial's baby' (Murungun *alpha*), 'Murungun, Purdal's baby' (Murungun *beta*), etc.

Which brings us, in a roundabout way, back to the question; Are these Mara social units patrilineal or not? All this about matri-determination suggests not, a conclusion supported by what Spencer and Gillen have to say about alternate marriages. Thus a Murungun *alpha* man should marry a Purdal *alpha* woman; but he may also marry a Kuial *alpha* woman 'if she come from a distant locality' (Spencer and Gillen, 1904, p. 126). This is analogous to the alternate marriages permitted in Arunta and Gidjingali with a 'cousin', or between individuals of classes 1 and

5. But unlike Arunta classes, membership in the Mara divisions is based on matrifiliation: the children of a Murungun *alpha* man and a Kuial *alpha* woman would not be Murungun *beta* but Mumbali *beta* (ibid., pp. 126-7). So much for 'patrilineal descent groups' in Mara culture (cf. Warner, 1933, pp. 78-83; Maddock, 1969b).

This is not to say that the constituent units of a semi-moiety system cannot really be patrilineal. Those of the Mara and their immediate neighbours are not; neither are the still better-documented schemes of the tribes further east on the Gulf of Carpentaria (Sharp, 1935), which probably provided the basis for Elkin's stereotype. But the four-part division of the Arunta is clearly based on patrifiliation, as is its Miwuyt analogue.

Semi-moiety organization in north-east Arnhem Land has a different foundation from the arrangements already discussed, though the product is similar (Shapiro, 1969b). Rather than consisting of four named units (as with the Mara), four couples with matrifiliation (eastern Gulf tribes), or four couples with patrifiliation (Arunta), it is an unnamed but direct division of the ritual lodges themselves. This division is accomplished by means of the relationship terminology, applied between lodges on the basis of mythic associations and independent of individual genealogical connections. Thus any lodge regards another lodge of its own moiety as either a 'sibling' or a 'mother's mother', whereas an opposite-moiety lodge is either a 'mother' or a 'woman's child'. Any two 'sibling' lodges are in identical positions in this scheme: a third lodge which is 'sibling' to one is 'sibling' to the other, a fourth which is 'mother' to one is 'mother' to the other, etc. The entire society is in this way divided into four sets of 'sibling' lodges.

Each set is assumed to be ritually distinct, and to carry on particular relationships with the other three sets. Opposite-moiety lodges are sources of wives and recipients of sisters: these need concern us no further. What should be emphasized, though, is the 'mother's mother' set, that is the other semi-moiety of one's own moiety: this is regarded as the source of mothers-in-law for the men of one's own set. And 'mother's mother' is here self-reciprocal: sisters move in both directions, and are converted into mothers-in-law in the process.

All this must seem bizarre, yet it is nothing more than what relates the two semi-moieties of a moiety among the Arunta, the Mara and other Gulf tribes, and probably in most of the rest of Aboriginal Australia. Later we shall see why the first Australians are even more preoccupied with their mothers-in-law than their European brethren are.

But first a scholastic retreat. I have so far suggested a broader notion of semi-moiety organization than Elkin's, one more in keeping with Radcliffe-Brown's: I first did this in an article published several years ago (Shapiro, 1967b). In the interim, the Australian anthropologist Kenneth Maddock (1969b, pp. 101-2, note 2) has taken issue with me:

> Shapiro . . . wishes to define the term 'semi-moiety' to cover systems consisting in a fourfold division into patrilineal clans . . ., as well as systems consisting in a fourfold division into . . . [couples in an eight-class scheme]. I find the proposed usage unfortunate, because it blurs the distinction between two types of quadripartite organization, which may both be found in one tribe. A consequence of alternative . . . [class] marriages is that two men belonging to the same 'semi-moiety', understood as a grouping of clans, may belong to different 'semi-moieties', understood as . . . [couples of classes]. Thus Shapiro's 'broader conceptualization of semi-moiety organization' conflates distinct social divisions.

The Dalabon of Central Arnhem Land (Map 1), studied by Maddock first-hand, exemplify a culture with 'two types of quadripartite organization': an eight-class system with the usual couples, and a fourfold division more or less identical to that of the Mara (plus ritual lodges which are apparently not grouped in the Miwuyt fashion) (Maddock, 1969a, 1969b, 1972a). A sound analysis of Dalabon culture (as Maddock's is) should make the distinctions that the Dalabon do: at this level, I would agree, my notion of semi-moiety organization is inadequate.[2] Yet surely it is no accident that, in a relatively small area centring

[2] This approach to ethnography is developed by Goodenough (1970) and Keesing (1966). See also the other articles by these authors in the bibliography of this book.

around the Gulf of Carpentaria (but extending to much of the rest of Australia), there are at least three structurally distinct realizations of a single, remarkably uniform pattern (Map 1).[3] Radcliffe-Brown had a glimmer of this. At the comparative level I think we should follow his lead and label this plan 'semi-moiety organization' wherever and in whatever form it occurs.

The pattern, we have seen, is a four-part scheme which contains certain affinal norms. It is also patrilineal—if not always in principle (Arunta, Miwuyt), at least in the looser sense of ideally 'coupling' father and son (Dalabon, Mara, eastern Gulf tribes). This is important; in all the cases discussed and others as well, semi-moieties are ceremonial units, and, as we have seen, ritual life in Aboriginal Australia is mainly a patrilineal concern. What semi-moiety organization seems to do is to create the notion that the ritual lodges and hence ritual life on the one hand and affinal norms on the other are parts of one and the same plan. This notion is false, or rather only partly true, because of the pervasive influence of 'matrilineal' ideas in Aboriginal social life: of, for example, matrifiliation in the Dalabon class system (Maddock, 1969b) and her matri-kin's rights over a girl's bestowal in Miwuyt marriage. But it may nonetheless be a construct fundamental to Aboriginal thought—much like those other cultural exaggerations, the linked dichotomies presented in chapter 4, and, less certainly, the logical structure unearthed in four- (and eight-?) class systems.

There are some cases of *matrilineal* semi-moiety organization, though none of these has been adequately documented (Berndt and Berndt, 1970, pp. 61-6; Stanner in Goody, 1961). But just their existence underlies a position which has so far been mostly implicit in this book, and to which I now turn more directly.

Most of this and the preceding chapter or two is heavily weighted with what Malinowski, master of intellectual politics, derogated as 'kinship algebra'; it seems to fall short of what that venerated racist called 'the real facts of savage life' (Malinowski,

---

[3] Just how widespread this pattern is is uncertain, though it seems safe to say that it exists wherever an eight-class system does. An approximate idea of its distribution can be gained from the map in Berndt and Berndt (1964, p. 56).

1930). A related *obiter dictum* on Aboriginal social classification has more recently been expressed by Robin Fox (1967a, p. 184):

> The joke is usually made that these natives have elaborated their kinship systems because there was not much else to do. There was in fact a good deal else to do—staying alive in fact; and the Australian was not the man to waste time elaborating a kinship system for the fun of it unless such a system had a high survival value.

I think we are entitled to ask how Fox knows that this last statement is true. As it stands, it is no more than a scholastic assertion based on a queer marriage of Darwin and Marx; it may (or may not) have an emotional appeal to some, but its connection with testable empirical propositions—the stuff of which science is made—is not at all clear.

Against this stance it could be argued that—contrary to popular (and apparently Fox's) opinion—most foragers, far from being perennially on the verge of starvation, have an entirely adequate, dependable, and easily exploited subsistence base, and consequently far more leisure time than most middle-class Europeans (Lee, 1968). To this could be added the fact that doing something for the fun of it—play—occurs among our primate and other mammalian cousins, and is thus presumably a part of the human animal (Hess, 1970).

These considerations make it easier to entertain the possibility that Aboriginal kinship indeed belongs to the realm of play, a notion which, as we have seen, A. L. Kroeber espoused. This possibility only opens doors (and minds): in itself it is no more demonstrable than Fox's pragmatist assertion. We need to know why Aborigines play the games they do, and the logical relations within and among these games. Kroeber, Lévi-Strauss, Scheffler, and others have addressed themselves primarily to the latter question, as I do here. The former, I suspect, is soluble mostly on historical grounds.[4]

---

[4] Historical explanations are sometimes held to be particularistic, i.e. to pertain to phenomena which occur in only one or at most a few instances, to answer the question 'How?' but not 'Why?' and therefore to be supplementary to other sorts of explanation. All these commonsense and absurdly outdated notions are exploded by Driver (1966) with reference to a particular anthropological problem.

If, in short, much of the foregoing is 'kinship algebra'—or as I would rather call it, 'cognitive play'—, then it is not only the anthropologist who is involved with it. Nor as play is it necessarily unserious (Huizinga, 1955, esp. pp. 5-6). Stanner's analysis of Murinbata social organization (pp. 68-70) is probably the best published exemplification of both these propositions. Any unsupported assertion that activity of this kind is something apart from 'the real facts of savage life' carries the curious assumption that aesthetic creativity is expectable only in the 'higher' civilizations, and the very definite stench of intellectual racism.

NINE

Some aspects of the conjugal bond

I have already said more than a little about affinity in Aboriginal Australia, though only in the context of other matters. I want to turn now more directly to this topic, particularly to certain aspects of the conjugal bond itself. Most of the issues raised here have been appreciated since the early decades of the last century, when the first reports of European explorers in Australia appeared.[1] Since then these issues have engendered more and better documentation but relatively little controversy.

The two things that most caught the fancy of the explorers are those that are obvious and remarkable to almost any European visitor: that *polygyny* is permitted, which is to say that a man may have more than one wife; and that the age difference between spouses is often marked—especially in favour of the husband—so that it is not uncommon for a pre-pubescent girl to be married to an aged codger. By contrast, no known Aboriginal culture permits *polyandry*—the marriage of a woman to more than one man. An Aboriginal woman may have only one husband at a time. Or, more accurately, she *must* have one and only one husband at a time, for she may not choose to be single.[2]

---

[1] For reviews of those reports germane to this essay, see Fry (1933, pp. 258-61), Malinowski (1913), and Thomas (1906). Thomas's book deserves special mention for its early and profound insights into Aboriginal social organization. In more ways than can be mentioned here it initiated Aboriginal anthropology into the twentieth century.

[2] Apart from recent changes, there are some exceptions reported in the literature. But all or most of these seem to involve older women, who characteristically are allowed far more freedom than their younger sisters, including the option of non-coresidence with their husbands. This, however, does not make them unmarried, unless we want to make coresidence a defining attribute of 'marriage'. This in turn would be a poor conceptual move, for we could no longer speak of 'marital separation'; and we should have to deal

In theory, at least, she is somebody's wife from womb to tomb (chapter 10).

But this 'somebody' need not be the same man throughout her life and will probably not be, especially because of the age difference noted above. A woman's first husband is nearly always much her senior; hence she will almost certainly outlive him. With his death, she will go to another man, ideally a brother or other 'sibling' of her first husband; the new man may also be much older and therefore also predecease her. *Et cetera.* Running through a line of husbands in this fashion will surely make the woman no younger; and the age difference between her and each successive husband will probably consistently decrease until her old age, when she may well be married to a man younger than herself.[3]

To the extent that polygyny without polyandry is practised and the sex ratio approaches 50:50, some men will necessarily be unmarried. As you may have inferred from my remarks on age differences between spouses, such a fate usually befalls younger men. This can be illustrated with data I obtained from several parts of the Miwuyt area. In the following tabulation, men are classed into two age categories—forty or over, and between twenty and forty—and by the number of wives they have, the range being from zero to seven.[4]

in other terms with the considerable number of societies in which husband and wife do not normally reside together (Alland, 1963; Fox, 1967a, pp. 37-40; Gough, 1959). Later in this chapter I return to the problem of an anthropological definition of 'marriage' and its relation to the Aboriginal data.

[3] Hart and Pilling (1960), in their monograph on the Tiwi, make the same points, but they support them only with impressionistic and arbitrarily selected data. A far more rigorous study of Tiwi marriage is that of Goodale (1971). The quantitative assertions in this section are based primarily upon Goodale's material; Frederick Rose's monumental study of the Wanindiljaugwa of Groote Eylandt (Rose, 1960; Map 1); Meggitt's statistical analysis of Walbiri marriage (1965); Long's compilations for various tribes (1970b); and my own as yet unpublished data from north-east Arnhem Land. Not all these assertions are supported by all of these studies, but I take the former to hold generally though not universally in Aboriginal Australia.

[4] These remarks require certain clarifications. First, the age dichotomy of men does not reflect a distinction made by the Miwuyt: it is entirely my own invention, though, as can be seen, it does elucidate certain regularities in their society. Second, females are counted as wives only if there is evidence (from their age or coresidence with their husbands) that the marriage has been consummated. Girls below the age of about twelve, though married

No. of men with	Age 40+	Age 20-39
7 wives	3	0
6 wives	0	0
5 wives	5	0
4 wives	3	1
3 wives	13	3
2 wives	20	10
1 wife	42	52
0 wife	4	40

In short, the 90 men forty years of age or over have a total of 179 wives—an average of almost exactly two wives per man—whereas the 106 men under forty have a total of 85 wives.[5]

Of particular interest are the 44 men without a wife, and the fact that nearly all of them are under forty. Of the four in my senior age category, three are widowers, whereas only one has never been married. By contrast, only one of the 40 single men under forty is a widower; the other 39 have always been single.

Such situations, general among Aborigines, are precarious. As Frederick Rose (1968, p. 207) has observed,

> . . . Australian aboriginal society is on the horns of a dilemma . . . This situation leads to the older men—past their physical and sexual peak—monopolizing the women in polygynous units. On the other hand, the younger men—at their physical and sexual peak—are virtually without women . . . This contradiction in Australian society has been resolved by the older men controlling the younger through the elaborate system of male initiation found in Australia.

in theory, usually do not reside with their husbands. This distinction, between 'actual wives' and 'promised wives', is made by the Miwuyt. Third, since Miwuyt dialects contain no word for a definite number greater than two, my age reckoning had to be made by external criteria; these are discussed in Shapiro (1970b, p. 66). Fourth (and related), the seven wives maximum is fortuitous and does not reflect a cultural limitation. Thus my later analysis of residence groups (Shapiro, 1973) revealed that one of the men in the tabulation with seven wives in fact has eight, and even higher numbers have been reported for other parts of north-east Arnhem Land (Berndt, 1965, pp. 87-8; Warner, 1937, p. 77).

[5] The greater number of females (264) than males (196) in this tabulation is due less to an unequal sex ratio than to certain cultural facts—that females can become 'actual wives' at about age twelve, whereas males cannot become 'actual husbands' until about age twenty.

Rose goes on to provide a useful list of common features of Aboriginal male initiation, at the same time respecting the secrets communicated in the ceremonies. I shall return to some of these features in the next chapter. But I must note here that, however gratifying and intimidating the initiation process is, it is by no means wholly effective in deterring young (and not-so-young) men from heterosexual satisfaction outside marriage. Hiatt's recent study of Gidjingali conflict provides only a sounder base for what we already knew impressionistically: that disputes involving sexual access to women are the major source of strife in Aboriginal communites (Hiatt, 1965, pp. 75-102, 105-12).

There are, however, two sorts of institutionalized means of sharing the wealth. One of these, which I shall gloss as 'sweet-heartship', may be illustrated by my Miwuyt data.

If a Miwuyt man, married or not, wants to carry on with another man's wife, he can signal his intent by placing a specially designed cord, otherwise used in ceremonial contexts, into her food-gathering container.[6] A woman so approached must be in the 'wife' category with respect to her would-be paramour, who, if successful, will refer to her as his *mangutji*—'hole'—an unromantic metaphor for 'vagina'. Thereafter, the man is supposed to bring gifts of food to his sweetheart, but the latter is not expected to reciprocate in kind. As one informant observed: 'I have to give food to her, not she to me; she's already "fed" me' (cf. p. 56, n. 3; Warner, 1937, pp. 79-90).

Now in Miwuyt culture, extramarital intercourse is regarded as improper; adulterous undertakings of the kind described are classed as 'left-handed' (*wingku*) and 'crooked' (*djarrpi*), as opposed to minding one's own yard, which is 'right-handed' and 'straight' (both *dunupa*).[7] That people in north-east Arnhem Land and elsewhere violate their own avowed notions of pro-

---

[6] There is evidence that the cord represents semen and the container its owner's vagina. I should also note that my data on Miwuyt 'sweetheartship', obtained as they were from male informants, are regrettably one-sided.

[7] The relation right: left:: proper: improper occurs in the semantics of English and other Indo-European languages, and in those of very many other languages as well; it is probably very close to being what some of us like to call a 'substantive cultural universal' (Chomsky, 1965, pp. 27-30; Greenberg, 1968, pp. 142-3; Needham, 1973b; cf. Miller,

priety is no surprise. But Miwuyt men and women not only defy the Seventh Commandment; around this defiance they have built an edifice of categories, rules, and standardized procedures—in short, a culture, or better (to borrow a term from pop sociology) a 'counter-culture'.

You hardly have to go to Arnhem Land to find counter-cultures; still, it is worth noting that these remarkable creations of the human mind are not confined to 'modern' societies. Sociologists have written about them for decades, mostly by interspersing some imposing statistics among some unimposing casual impressions and intuitions. Cultural anthropologists have barely studied them at all.

The other institution of interest here is best exemplified by a custom called *pirrauru*, practised by the Dieri and neighbouring tribes of South Australia (Map 1). The *pirrauru* relationship can exist only between a man and a woman who are in 'spouse' categories with respect to each other, and it further resembles Dieri 'marriage' in that both sexual and economic services are involved. It differs from 'marriage' (*tippa-malku*) in that cohabitation is necessarily only temporary, and there is no affinal relationship established between the man and the woman's cognates. Rather, the initiative in arranging a *pirrauru* relationship is supposed to be taken by the woman's husband, who may present her to either a married or an unmarried man, or both, or any combination of appropriately related men, and who in any case does not lose his rights to his wife or his obligations to her cognates.

Dieri 'marriage' is exclusive: a woman will have many men who stand in the 'spouse' category to her, but with only one of these, at any one time, may she have a *tippa-malku* relationship. By contrast, it can be seen that *pirrauru* rules are far more permissive, and the resultant relationships overlap. There is no theoretical limit to the number of *pirrauru* a woman may have, and she may share some or all of them with one or more other

1972). Straight: crooked:: proper: improper is also widespread, both in the Indo-European family and elsewhere; but, because of inadequate attention from anthropologists, its status as a possible near-universal is uncertain.

women. Which is also to say that a man may have several *pirrauru*, to none of whom he has exclusive rights. (Howitt, 1891, pp. 53-63, 1904, pp. 181-7; Elkin, 1938b, pp. 75-7).

It is these last considerations, so appealing to modern buffs of conjugal experimentation, that also, ironically, engaged a generation of Victorian social theory. Nineteenth century anthropology was much taken with the notion of 'group marriage', which was supposed to have been an early characteristic of human social life everywhere, and of which *pirrauru* and similar institutions were thought to be survivals. Shortly after the turn of the century, most of this edifice of theory was demolished by Northcote Thomas (1906, pp. 102-49)—so thoroughly that Malinowski's more famous dissection of 'group marriage' in Aboriginal Australia, published seven years later, was little more than a *post-mortem* (Malinowski, 1913, esp. pp. 108-23; see also Lang, 1903, pp. 89-111, 1905, pp. 38-58; Korn, 1973, pp. 48-51). More recently, the idea has had a minor renaissance within anthropology (de Leeuwe, 1963; Gough, 1959), and it may even be properly applicable to a few social situations; but the significance attached to it by Morgan (1877) and others is entirely discredited.

The ethnographic task here, please note, is only to distinguish *pirrauru* from *tippa-malku*—because the Dieri do. So far as I know, the Dieri do not worry about which of their institutions should be called 'marriage'. Rather, this is a job for comparison-minded anthropologists; and most of those who have tackled it seriously in recent years would presumably conclude that *tippa-malku* is marriage but *pirrauru* not—just as Lang, Thomas, and Malinowski did more than a half-century ago (Crocker, 1969a; Goodenough, 1970, pp. 6-17; Gough, 1959, cf. Leach, 1961c, ch. 4; Rivière, 1971). Note too that this is precisely the sort of division of anthropological labour we encountered in the last chapter, in dealing with semi-moiety organization.

TEN

The wider network of affinity

One approach to Aboriginal affinity derives from Lévi-Strauss' *The elementary structures of kinship* (1969a), first published in French in 1949. Lévi-Strauss has never carried out ethnographic research in Australia nor, as we shall see, does he suffer from overfamiliarity with the published Aboriginal materials; and the same can be said for most of those—Fox (1967a, pp. 175-239), Leach (1961c, ch. 3), Livingstone (1959), and Needham (1962), among others—who have advanced his views. Nevertheless their cumulative effect on the uninitiated has been mesmerizing and needs to be dispelled.[1]

Supporters of Lévi-Strauss' scheme do not all say the same thing, and in recent years some of them have all but abandoned the Captain's Ship or at least drastically remodelled it (Dumont, 1971; Fox, 1972; Maddock, 1969a; Needham, 1973a). Still, I think it can be shown that the bulk of their writing makes the following assumptions about Aboriginal social organizations:

1) Ritual lodges are united in themselves and distinguished from each other by patrilocal residence.

2) Ritual lodges, so distinguished, are allied with each other

---

[1] Berndt (1955), on the basis of his own work in north-east Arnhem Land, has attempted to apply Lévi-Strauss to Miwuyt marriage. Radcliffe-Brown (1956) was quick to show the internal inconsistencies in Berndt's analysis, and I have collected data which lend themselves to very different interpretations (Shapiro, 1968, 1969a, 1969b). There is, in fact, a very large number of critiques of Lévi-Strauss on particular issues, as well as a small but effective literature, discussed below, which disposes of most of his notions about Aboriginal marriage. But the most fundamental and devastating attacks on his general scheme are those of Harold Scheffler (esp. 1970, 1973b, pp. 780-6), with which any serious student of the subject must be familiar.

through marriage. This is the Aboriginal version of the corner-
stone of the Lévi-Straussian approach. Yet it is far from clear
what 'alliance' is supposed to mean here and how its presence is
supposed to be gauged. The marital-political alliances of, for
example, historic European nobility were self-conscious and
usually explicit in their intent, but there is nothing comparable
recorded for Aboriginal Australia. Anthropologists often speak
of individual marriages as 'creating' or 're-affirming' or
'strengthening' alliances between groups, but they usually offer
no supporting evidence. I consider such utterances to be platitudes, or else not-too-subtle tautologies in which 'marriage' and
'alliance' are synonymous. I take this up again below.

3) Because marriage thus has implications for entire groups,
ritual lodges act corporately in arranging individual marriages.
This means that the older males (see the following assumption)
of the intermarrying lodges negotiate the union, or at a mini-
mum, that females are bestowed in marriage by their fathers. The
Lévi-Straussian commitment to this assumption is so solemn that
when an American female anthropologist (Lane, 1961) dared to
suggest as a hypothetical possibility that women in a society with
patrilineal groups might be bestowed by their matrikin, she was
summarily trodden upon by two members of the Continental
Cavalry (Leach, 1961a; Needham, 1963; cf. Lane, 1962). And
when Hiatt (1968) showed that such an arrangement actually
exists—in Aboriginal Australia no less—Lévi-Strauss himself
came up with the profound retort that European influence
obviates taking the case seriously (see the exchange—surely not
an alliance—between Hiatt and Lévi-Strauss in Lee and DeVore,
1968, pp. 210-12).

4) In such inter-lodge relationships, there is a sexual division
of function, such that females are the objects by which the
relationships are signalled, males the givers and recipients of
these objects. Which is to say that males are never themselves
objects, nor females ever agents. Feminists will find this offensive.
An incidental consideration, discussed below, is that it is also
false.

5) These relationships involve not only alliance but exchange
as well: if one ritual lodge gives a woman in marriage to another,

the latter is supposed to reciprocate. This assumption is based in turn almost entirely on certain notions about Aboriginal relationship terminologies: (a) that they consist of patri-sequences; (b) that each of these sequences corresponds, for any Ego, to one (or more?) ritual lodges, in both native theory and reality; and (c) that Ego's lodge is a 'spouse' lodge to his 'spouse' lodge—that is that 'spouse' terms are self-reciprocal. But even if all these subordinate assumptions were invariably true, marital exchange would be entailed only if Ego had one and only one 'spouse' lodge. Though Lévi-Straussians usually deny that they subscribe to this restrictive possibility, their insistence on reciprocity, coupled with their ignorance of extra-terminological evidence, would appear to make it essential to their scheme.[2] Hence:

6) The size of such alliance/exchange networks is dependent upon the number of patri-sequences in the associated relationship terminology. Thus these networks among the Arunta and the Gidjingali embrace four lodges, or at least more lodges than are involved in networks associated with two-sequence terminologies, and are therefore said to entail a higher degree of social integration. Note that this is true by definition: no independent evidence for integration is given (cf. assumption 2).

This set of assumptions yields a model of spatially distinct groups, each, through marriage, collectively engaged in alliance/exchange relations with other such groups. The picture is appealing, even poetic: a Paleolithic United Nations, the very dawn of diplomacy (Fox, 1967a, pp. 175-84; Tiger and Fox, 1971, pp. 88-9).

Though the prosaic facts had been around for some time, they remained unsynthesized and their theoretical significance unappreciated until the 1960s. These relatively thankless but seminal tasks were taken up mostly by L. R. Hiatt. Assumption (1) was first to go: it squared neither with Hiatt's Gidjingali data nor with such other materials as were available in 1962 (p. 23). Three years later Hiatt published a major monograph on his

---

[2] I suspect that the Lévi-Straussians have become victims of their diagrams, which I thus assiduously avoid here.

work in north-central Arnhem Land, in which he presented these as two of his most salient findings:

> . . . Radcliffe-Brown's generalizations about Aboriginal local organization did not apply to the Gidjingali. These people lived not in separate patrilineal patrilocal hordes but in [multi-lodge] communities . . . [And] patrilineal groups were not units in wife-exchange systems of the kind implied by Lévi-Strauss's theory on kinship and marriage (Hiatt, 1965, p. xiv).

Rather, said Hiatt, 'A woman and her brothers had a joint right to bestow her daughters in marriage' (p. 41), that is a girl is bestowed by her matrikin, both male and female.

> A woman could bestow her daughter as early as the crawling stage. If she had brothers, the future husband was chosen in consultation with them . . . [But] people discussing rules of bestowal often referred only to the girl's mother. . . . A father did not share the right to give his daughter. He often tried to influence his wife, but she was not obliged to heed him. The Gidjingali said that on this occasion 'the father is nothing' (pp. 42-44).

Hiatt went on to represent Gidjingali relationship terms in the form of 'a hypothetical closed system of [affinal] relationships among four patrilineal groups'; but this was no more than a diagrammatic convenience, for 'no system of this kind was proposed by the people as an ideal, nor did it occur in practice' (p. 44).

Another three years culminated in a restatement of these findings, with more deliberate attention to their bearing on the Lévi-Straussian model:

> Patriclans . . . as corporate groups had nothing to do with the [bestowal] decision, and there was no rule or ideal saying that they ought to. A model of marriage-exchange using these groups as units departs seriously from reality. . . . Gidjingali men did not have rights to give their . . . daughters in marriage (Hiatt, 1968, p. 174).

Which occasioned the sorry response from Lévi-Strauss already noted. But Hiatt's findings are by no means unusual. I have already called attention to a similar setup in Miwuyt culture, and I have alluded to its generality in Aboriginal

Australia. My first effort in this direction was in 1966, in an unpublished paper which was circulated within the narrow clique of Aboriginal kinship buffs. Hiatt, in what is probably the most important review of Aboriginal affinity ever written, was kind enough to note it:

> The point I am making . . . has been made already by Shapiro . . . After drawing attention to evidence of the type I have presented above, Shapiro concludes that '. . . patrilineal societies in which a woman's disposal in marriage is partially or entirely in the hands of individuals outside her own [patri] sib not only exist in Australia, they abound.' . . . The task now . . . is to make some sense of this fact. . . . I offer the following . . . considerations . . . there is a widespread notion in Australia that an individual's flesh is transmitted matrilineally, his spirit patrilineally . . . A man is not importantly concerned in the fleshly aspect of procreation. Usually he is supposed to dream that a 'child-spirit' enters his wife's womb, and this belief is typically an integral part of patrilineal descent group ideology . . . We might argue, then, that, as females have a high fleshly status but a low spiritual status, it is seen as appropriate that their disposal in marriage should be the business of their matrikin. Put another way, when a girl is bestowed in marriage, it is her body that is given, not her spirit. It is proper that those responsible for her flesh should be the ones with the right to dispose of it. (Hiatt, 1967, p. 473).

This harks back to much that we discussed earlier, especially in chapter 4. Now Hiatt's analysis was prompted by a review by Fox of Meggitt's Walbiri monograph, in which bestowal is summarized as follows:

> A woman's own matriline . . . actively give her in marriage. Although her father is also concerned, it is as an individual, apart from his own matri- or patri-line. Conversely, a man is more concerned with the matriline from which he receives a wife . . . (Meggitt, 1962, p. 195).[3]

I presume this last sentence to mean that a Walbiri man is supposed to be more concerned with his wife's matriline than

---

[3] For present purposes, the following translations will do: Meggitt's 'matriline' = matrikin; 'patriline' = ritual lodge.

with her father. Anyway, the last-named would appear to be more important in bestowal than his Gidjingali counterpart (but see p. 99 *et seq.*). But Fox (1967b, p. 329) is hardly entitled to conclude from this that 'The alliance is obviously between two patri-units', or indeed that there's an 'alliance' at all; and that the wife's matriline is simply a lackey for her ritual lodge: 'One could view the whole system as an expression of the alliance between patrilodges . . ., with the matrilines . . . as the appropriate functionaries in the actual arrangement of the marriage.'

One could, but do the Walbiri? It seems clear from his response to Hiatt that Fox does not think it necessary to bother with such small matters:

> What Hiatt takes . . . [my position] to mean and what I unwittingly seem to have suggested as its sole meaning is something like *the analysis of formal relationships between formal groups expressed in the formal exchange or circulation of women between these groups.* He rightly points out, as have other Australianists, that this is not what happens . . . What throws the whole issue into confusion is the tendency of 'alliance' writers (and I am also to blame) to write 'as if' this were what happened. Thus, in examining the formal properties of a system, one says 'Group A exchanges women with Group B,' or 'Group A gives a woman to Group B and hence expects Group B to reciprocate at a later date', and the like. . . . [Yet] it is perfectly true that no clan . . . in Australia ever gets together as a formal unit, hands over a woman to another clan . . ., and demands another woman in return . . . But . . . the nature of the rules ensures that women will pass . . . between . . . clans . . . (Fox, 1969, pp. 15-16; emphases in original).

We are thus asked to believe that Fox and Hiatt are not at odds at all, but merely have different interests in the same data:

> I was not concerned with who had the actual rights of . . . bestowal . . . What I was stressing was the fact that the movement of women in marriage mediated relationships, or, if you prefer, 'expressed' relationships, between clans . . . (ibid., p. 15).

But is there any ethnographic substance in this last statement? Suppose I, a brown-eyed American Jew, were to marry a blue-eyed Englishwoman and 'move' her to New York. Would NATO be strengthened? What would happen (because of ties to my ancestral estate) to Anglo-Israeli relations? Not much, I think. Yet surely relationships between brown-eyed people and blue-eyed people would be mediated—or, if you prefer, 'expressed'.

Lévi-Straussian assumption (1) was tackled in chapter 3. So far most of the present section has been devoted to assumptions (2) and (3). As for assumption (4) and its corollary, I have already quoted Hiatt on the authority of Gidjingali women in bestowing their daughters; and I have now to add, following Hiatt (1967), that this is general among Aborigines. The converse situation—the conceptualization and use of males as objects—is best exemplified in the sphere of ritual. It rests on the profound parallel in Aboriginal thought between the marital life of females and the ritual life of males.

One of these parallels entails the premise that circumcision, usually the first step in a man's ceremonial career, is equivalent to a girl's first menstrual flow, the beginning of her active married life. Thus a boy is symbolically cast out of the circle of his primary kin before he is cut, and in at least some tribes is said to be 'given' to his initiators—just as a girl at about the same time of life is 'given' to her husband (Beckett, 1967; Rose, 1968).

This parallel is carried to the point where circumcision itself is part of the complex of affinal rights and obligations. Thus in many areas a boy's proper circumciser is his potential father-in-law, that is a man of the 'wife's father' category, whose daughter is considered appropriate compensation for the ordeal.[4] Here, it would seem, conceptually equivalent objects—the girl's sexual capacities and the boy's foreskin—are seen as mutually exchangeable.[5]

Probably even more common is the role of a boy's sister's husband as what has been called his 'ritual guardian'. Frederick

---

[4] Note that this implies only that men lose their daughters to the boys they circumcize, not that men have bestowal rights over their daughters. This is considered below (pp. 110-12) in more detail.

[5] There is in fact more direct evidence for this, but its presentation would involve undue revelation of sacred materials.

Rose has provided us with a general description of this role, with special reference to the Wanindiljaugwa of Groote Eylandt:

> . . . during part of his initiation extending over some years, a youth is attached to, and is under the strict control and tutelate of . . ., a considerably older man. This guardian is frequently the youth's sister's husband . . . He not only has the responsibility of continuing by practical example the instruction of the initiate in the hunting of game and the other manly arts, but he also has rights to dispose of what foodstuffs the initiate brings back to camp. *The guardian's interest in controlling an initiate is not greatly dissimilar to his interest in controlling the initiate's sister as wife.* It is indicative of the relationship existing between initiate and guardian that on Groote Eylandt the missionaries frequently referred to the initiate . . . as a 'boy wife'. Stealing of young wives from their husbands was a feature of traditional life on Groote Eylandt, and it is significant that initiates were stolen in the same way . . . from their guardians . . . (Rose, 1968, p. 207; emphases added).

A gay affair? With wives so hard to come by, one might expect homosexuality to be rampant in Aboriginal Australia. But this does not appear to be the case. Thus Hiatt, in an unexpurgated (and unpublished) report to the Australian Institute of Aboriginal Studies, has shown that Gidjingali men are anything but libertines, and that their erotic horizons are quite limited (cf. Berndt and Berndt, 1951, p. 67). The Wanindiljaugwa may be less prudish; but I suspect that, throughout Australia, what is more important in attracting older men to younger ones is the prestige accruing to the 'ritual guardian' and other ceremonial statuses. A more conclusive factor is that a potential guardian may have little choice: he may owe his services to his wife's brother as an affinal duty to the latter's parents and other senior kin.

Incidentally, the age difference between guardian and initiate may at first blush appear strange, since in our experience brothers-in-law are more or less coeval. But in Aboriginal Australia, as we saw in the last chapter, a young man's sister is very often the wife of a much older man.

The conceptualization of males as objects in Aboriginal culture thus entails a broader view of affinity than is generally taken,

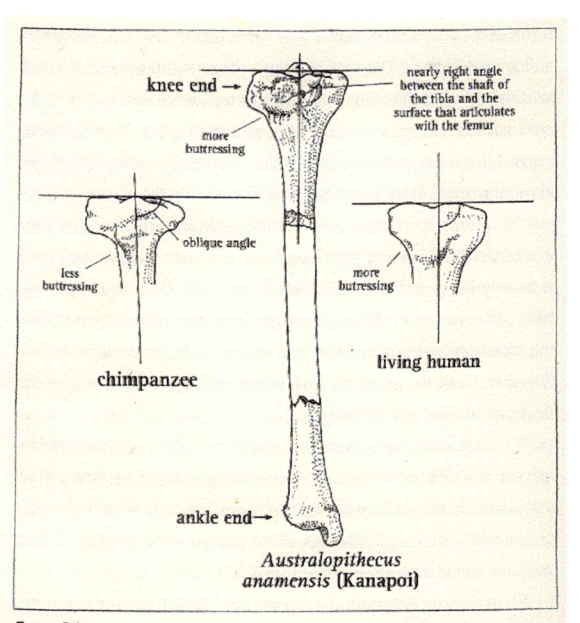

knee end →

nearly right angle
between the shaft of
the tibia and the
surface that articulates
with the femur

more
buttressing

oblique angle

less
buttressing

more
buttressing

chimpanzee

living human

*Australopithecus
anamensis* (Kanapoi)

ankle end →

FIGURE 2.6

Front views of tibias (shin bones) of a chimpanzee, *Australopithecus anamensis*, and of a living human (redrawn after M. G. Leakey 1995, *National Geographic* 190 (9), p. 45).

even by most anthropologists. A glimmer of just how wide a sphere of social and conceptual relations may have to be considered was given by A. P. Elkin over forty years ago, in a tantalizingly brief account of 'indebtedness' (*kopara*) among the Dieri and their neighbours:

> The exchange [in which the concept of *kopara* figures] may refer to gifts, women, lives, injuries, or initiation rites. The native word is used both as an adjective and a noun. In one sense, a *kopara* is a debt which must be settled in a definite standardized manner according to its nature. Thus, an individual or rather, . . . his matrilineal . . . clan—acquires a *kopara* against another person and his group in one of the following ways: (1) gifts have been made to the latter, but no reciprocal gifts have been received; (2) a man of one clan has received a woman in marriage from another clan, but has not arranged for the gift of a sister or sister's child in return; (3) the death of a member of one clan has been traced . . . to another clan, but has not been balanced either by the death of one of the latter . . ., by the gift of a wife, or by making one of the 'murderer's' clan *wilyaru*, that is, a fully initiated man; or (4) a member of one clan has been circumcised by a man of another clan, against whom he now has an obligation which may be settled by the gift of a wife. (Elkin, 1931a, p. 191).

Elkin adds that a *kopara* involving a gift—that is type (1)—can be settled by presenting to the creditor's group a kinswoman as a wife, and vice versa: a type (2) *kopara* can be settled by a gift (p. 192). We thus presumably have a conceptual equivalence, based on equivalence in exchange, among a series of objects:

gifts = females = human lives = boy's foreskin = *wilyaru* initiation

Note that the agents in this exchange scheme are said to be matrilineal groups, not ritual lodges, even for sacred activities such as circumcision. But Elkin (ibid.) quickly adds that a man can enter into or fulfil a *kopara* relationship not only by the presentation of his sister or sister's daughter, but by that of his daughter as well. Whether he has bestowal rights over the last-named is unclear, and in any case need not concern us here. What is more germane is that a man's daughter is *not* a member of his matrilineal group. This suggests that such groups are not really exchange units; and that the parties in *kopara* links are effectively defined by their kin relationship to one another, not by group membership.

Similarly, my Miwuyt informants often discussed actual or hypothetical marriages in a ritual lodge idiom—'A man of lodge A has married, or could marry, a woman of lodge B'—yet the marriage was or should be effected by the woman's matrikin. Other situations, such as fights or temporary camps, in which members of a certain lodge or lodges were numerically preponderant or otherwise conspicuous, were generally treated in the same idiom; but participation was governed by considerations of kindred rather than group (cf. Hiatt, 1965, pp. 131-41; Shapiro, 1973; on the kindred/kin-group distinction, see Goodenough, 1970, pp. 39-67).

I suspect that Elkin got comparable statements from his Dieri informants, and that he failed, despite the hints contravening their face value, to follow up these remarks. Why the Dieri, who also have ritual lodges, should choose a matrilineal idiom to express such relationships, I cannot say, but surely this is a secondary consideration. What is important, I think, is this: People everywhere use social categories to talk about social activities; but to assume therefore that membership in any particular category is either a necessary or a sufficient condition for participation in an associated activity is, without additional information, sheer nonsense (Goodenough, 1951, pp. 111-19, 1965; Keesing, 1969).

Nineteenth century anthropologists made this mistake when they inferred group marriage from the way Aborigines talk about their marriage-class schemes. The argument went something like this: If a man of class 1 could marry a woman of class 7, then any man of class 1 could marry that woman, and any other woman of her class. Such fine distinctions as whether or not the woman already had a husband were ignored. Few Western anthropologists today take this argument seriously.[6] Yet Lévi-Strauss and

---

[6] The notion of group marriage is, however, earnestly entertained in the Communist world, where, through Engels' assimilation of Morgan (1877) and Fison and Howitt (1880), it has become part of orthodox Marxist theory (Engels, 1942, 1st ed. 1884).

his followers, in their insistence that lodges or lodge-like groups act corporately in arranging marriages, are among our century's heirs to this tradition of ethnographic naiveté.

It should now be obvious that the Lévi-Straussian approach to Aboriginal affinity is untenable. Its use of such notions as 'alliance' and 'integration' constitutes little more than a tautological trap—a set of definitions masquerading as empirical propositions. Assumptions (1), (3), and (4), though directly testable, are probably false. So too is assumption (5), 'operationalized' in the form of propositions about relationship terminologies. As for assumption (6), we have very little evidence, and it is negative (Hiatt, 1965, pp. 130-1; Needham, 1962, pp. 244-6; Shapiro, 1969a, pp. 157-81, 1969b, pp. 634-6).

Now, with the bogus of 'alliance' behind us, we can more profitably look at Aboriginal affinity.

Since Aboriginal girls are bestowed by their maternal relatives, it should come as no surprise that one of the commonest kinds of exchange relationship involves affinal reciprocity between two sets of matrikin. The Dieri case has already been noted, but more interesting is the existence of similar arrangements in cultures lacking matrilineal groups. Hiatt (1967) has reviewed some of the literature on the most usual variety of this relationship in such cultures, in which two men are said to bestow upon each other their sister's daughters; Maddock (1969a) has added to this literature; and I found a variation of the theme in north-east Arnhem Land (Shapiro, 1968).

So far, for expository purposes, I have argued categorically for a 'matrilineal' view of bestowal. Though I consider this to be a general property of Aboriginal affinity, it has to be noted that matters are not really so simple. We have already seen that Walbiri fathers play a part in their daughters' bestowals, and that a Dieri man may give his daughter, or at least arrange for her to be given, in a *kopara* relationship. As for the Gidjingali, among whom, allegedly, 'the father is nothing' when it comes to bestowal, we have the following from Hiatt:

The Gidjingali say explicitly that a man does not have the right to choose his daughter's husband; yet several men told me that they had done just that. When I said that I was under the impression that the girl's [matrikin] had the right to bestow her, these men replied: 'Oh, yes, that's true, but her [matrikin] were quite happy about my choice' (1967, p. 474).

Hiatt further observes that 'There is . . . a good deal of equivocation and inconsistency in the ethnography on the question whether control of a girl's marital destiny is vested in her patrikin or her matrikin' (pp. 468-9), and proceeds to give several examples. Relating this to his Gidjingali findings, he reaches the following seminal conclusion:

> I would . . . suggest that, in practice, there is often a good deal of manoeuvring among a girl's close kin for effective control over her disposal . . . it may be reasonable to infer that some of the apparent inconsistency in earlier accounts of bestowal rights is really a record of equivocation among the natives, the occurrence and significance of which were not realized by the observers
> (pp. 473-4).

Peterson (1969, 1970a) has followed up on these suggestions for the Walbiri, as has Beckett (1967) for the Maljangaba of New South Wales (Map 1) and, from a different angle, Hamilton (1970) and I (Shapiro, 1969a, pp. 99-112) for the Gidjingali and Miwuyt, respectively. Hamilton's analysis is particularly revealing and will be considered in detail later. Right now, though, I want to call attention to the striking parallel between these materials, all of which stress paternal interest in bestowing daughters, and the systematic attempts by Aboriginal fathers to influence the lodge membership of their sons. On the whole these latter attempts seem to be more successful: Aboriginal Australians consider it more appropriate that men control the ritual life of their sons than the marital life of their daughters. But in both arenas they have no little difficulty keeping good men down.

One could conjecture that the facts just adduced suggest an historical sequence in the politics of Aboriginal marriage: an initial stage of exclusively 'matrilineal' authority; followed by the quick appearance of paternal influence at the 'subinstitutional' level, such as Hiatt reports for the Gidjingali; followed by the

'institutionalization' of this influence and its co-existence, perhaps in Walbiri fashion, with 'matrilineal' authority; and culminated, if not by the Advent of Christian Family Life, then at
least by an entirely paternal regime, such as may or may not exist
in Aboriginal Australia.

Whatever it is worth, this is hardly a new line of speculation.
Except for being informed by the social psychology of George
Homans (1961), and by the sad truth that Britannia Rules the
Waves no longer, it is just the sort of game Victorian social theory
played with the ethnography of the last century. Morgan (1877)
was its outstanding player in the United States, Lowie (1920,
pp. 147-85) the chief spoil-sport. A spectre survives, in distorted
form, in certain areas of psychoanalysis, the classics, and—most
recently—in the Women's Movement. Within anthropology a
more modest version of the theory has been resurrected, thanks
largely to the painstaking cross-cultural research of G. P. Murdock (1937, 1949, pp. 184-259, 1959a, pp. 377-8, 1959b; see
also Aberle, 1961).

Less careful writers on the subject fail to make a number of
empirically valid distinctions, among them that between principles governing the allocation of authority and principles
governing group membership. This is an especially important
consideration in dealing with the Aboriginal materials: Gidjingali social theory, for example, has girls bestowed by their
matrikin, but group membership is apparently based exclusively
on paternal connection. Elkin (1963, pp. 92-5) has argued—
correctly to my mind—that authority is founded on a common
set of elements everywhere in Aboriginal Australia, and that
these are independent of the principles of group composition.

I have saved for last the most striking aspect of Aboriginal
affinity—most striking for both us and the Aborigines. This has
to do with the relationship between son-in-law and mother-in-
law, and particularly with the way by which this bond is forged.
The contrast between our standards and theirs is probably
nowhere more marked than this: We have mothers-in-law
because we marry women's daughters, whereas Aboriginal men
have wives because they acquire their mothers.

One of the most pregnant statements in the entire literature on Aboriginal Australia is Elkin's, 'The tendency amongst the Australian Aborigines is to select the mother-in-law rather than the wife . . .' (1938b, p. 432; see also Radcliffe-Brown, 1951, p. 41). Its first substantial support came from Spencer and Gillen's classic, *The native tribes of Central Australia:*

> The . . . most usual method of obtaining a wife is that which is connected with the . . . custom in accordance with which every woman in the [Arunta] tribe is made *Tualcha mura* with some man. . . . it will be seen that, owing to a girl being made *Tualcha mura* to a boy of her own age, the men very frequently have wives much younger than themselves, as the husband and the mother of a wife obtained in this way are usually of approximately the same age.
>
> When it has been agreed upon between two men that the relationship shall be established between their two children, one a boy and the other a girl, the two latter . . . are taken to the . . . women's camp, and here each mother takes the other's child and rubs it all over with a mixture of fat and red ochre in the presence of all the other women, who have assembled for the purpose of watching the ceremony. At the same time some of the girl's hair is cut off and given to the boy to signalize the fact that when grown up it will be her duty to provide him (he will be her son-in-law) with her own hair from which to make his waist-girdles. The arrangement is . . . only made between boys and girls who stand in a definite relationship to one another. The girl must be one who is *Mura* ['wife's mother'] to the boy—that is, one whose daughters belong to the class from which his wife must come—but whilst, in common with all the women of her particular class she is already *Mura* to him, she now becomes *Tualcha mura*—that is, she is his actual or prospective mother-in-law. This relationship indicates that the man has the right to take as wife the daughter of the woman . . . (1899, pp. 558-9; also Spencer and Gillen, 1927, pp. 469-70).

In thus acquiring a *tualcha mura*, an Arunta man takes a calculated risk. At best, he will have to wait several years until she matures, is effectively married (perhaps to the man to whom *her* mother is *tualcha mura*), and bears and rears a daughter. At worst the would-be mother-in-law may be barren. Especially noteworthy is the obvious third possibility, in which her first child is a boy rather than the hoped-for wife. In that case the man may choose to become the boy's 'ritual guardian'. In the words of Spencer and Gillen (1899, pp. 559-60):

> This establishes a relationship between the boy and the man, as a result of which the former has, until he becomes . . . circumcised, to give his hair to the man who, on his part, has to, in a certain way, look after the boy; for example, he must grease his body occasionally and paint the sacred designs upon him at the . . . first of the initiatory rites. At . . . circumcision, the man has to tie the hair of the boy . . . and place the hair-girdle round his waist (also Spencer and Gillen, 1927, p. 470).[7]

This looks like a variant of the brother-in-law relationship noted earlier. The salient difference is that in claiming the son of his *tualcha mura* as his ward, our man must waive conjugal rights to any daughters she may later bear. Which is to say that a marital relationship with a female can be exchanged for a ritual relationship with a male—a notion whose remarkable implications we have already considered.

But to return to more mundane matters: Note that getting a wife in *tualcha mura* fashion entails not only a long wait on the part of the man but also a substantial age difference between conjugal partners. In north-east Arnhem Land and other areas a man of *any* age may thus acquire a mother-in-law, and this difference may accordingly be even greater. All of which goes a long way toward explaining why Aboriginal men are so often so much older than their wives, and why most young men are effectively unmarried.

Jane Goodale's studies of Tiwi marriage (Goodale, 1962, 1971) provide the richest published documentation of such a state of affairs. The focal event in the Tiwi case takes place

> . . . during the . . . period in which a girl is isolated . . . at the time of her first menstrual period. . . . she is not only considered to have reached the status of a woman but also that of a mother-in-law.

---

[7] In Arunta and many other cultures, hair seems to represent sexual potency (Leach, 1958). Fat (grease) and red ochre have much the same significance throughout Aboriginal Australia.

. . . her father places a spear between her legs as she sleeps and then presents it to a boy or man whom he selects to serve his daughter as a son-in-law. The spear is regarded by the recipient as a symbol of a bestowed wife yet to be born to his young mother-in-law. By accepting the spear, the son-in-law becomes obligated to his mother-in-law; from that moment on he must supply her with food and goods and such services as she may request at any time. In return, she is held solely responsible for seeing that her first daughter is sent to his camp when she reaches the wifely age of eight or ten. After receiving the first daughter, the son-in-law is expected to continue his services to his wife's mother, in return for which he can expect to receive other daughters subsequently born to her (Goodale, 1962, p. 454).

This last possibility runs counter to Arunta rules, according to which a *tualcha mura* woman presents only her first daughter to her son-in-law (Spencer and Gillen, 1899, p. 559). It is, however, consistent with Miwuyt procedures, and the preference for sororal polygyny in most of Aboriginal Australia suggests its generality. This in turn helps us understand why Aboriginal women not only go to older men, but go to them in bunches.

Also unlike Arunta, but like Miwuyt, Tiwi men are old enough, when they enter into the son-in-law/mother-in-law relationship, to do so independently, at least in theory without the authority of their elders. But in no case can the girl, at the initiation of the relationship, act on her own. In north-east Arnhem Land she is said to be 'given' and 'promised' to her son-in-law, who 'acquires' her. I shall therefore speak of 'mother-in-law bestowal' (Shapiro, 1969b, 1970b). Keep in mind that the 'mother-in-law' in question is a wife's mother, not a husband's, and that her position stems from her potential, not actual, maternity.

Among the subsidiary transactions in this most important of affinal relationships, we have already observed the Arunta mother-in-law's giving of her hair and the Tiwi son-in-law's prestation of (unspecified) food. This latter may be part of one of the commonest kinds of exchange in Aboriginal Australia: the movement of vegetable food from mother-in-law to son-in-law and of meat in the opposite direction. Probably all Aboriginal cultures distinguish between the two sorts of food and form with this distinction a metaphorical pairing: a symbolic association of vegetables with femininity and of meat with masculinity.[8]

Writing of the Walbiri, Nancy Munn puts this transaction in a larger context:

> As members of one family camp, a man and his wife (or wives) are said to share 'one sleep'. The reciprocal structure of their relationship is also expressed in Walbiri emphasis upon the food exchanges that take place between them: the husband is said to give his wife meat (*guyu*) and the woman to give him vegetable food (*miyi*...). This exchange is part of the wider system of exchanges between affines. A man is expected to give meat to his mother-in-law, while a mother-in-law should give vegetable food . . . to her son-in-law . . . The bonds of food exchange provide a constant symbolism expressing the affinal bond within the family and between a man and his wife's family. (1973, p. 10).

Such identification of wife and mother-in-law seems to be general in Aboriginal Australia and is expressed in several ways. I have already noted the sexual symbolism in the mother-in-law/son-in-law relationship in Arunta; and the Tiwi practice of bestowing a wife's mother by placing a spear between her legs hardly requires comment. In north-east Arnhem Land a young mother-in-law is ceremonially attached to a man when the latter places body grease (see p. 103, n. 7) into her navel, which according to local metaphor represents her vagina. And the same point is made, if more prosaically, by referring to a woman by the name of her mother's ritual lodge.

Erotic attitudes toward the mother-in-law have to be at least partially disguised: their more overt expression would run counter to one of the salient themes in her relationship with her son-in-law. Which brings us to the meaty question of affinal avoidances. Elkin's summary statement will do nicely:

> The severest taboo is that which is observed all over Australia

---

[8] Recall that vegetable food is gathered by women, whereas game is hunted by men. The symbolic associations of these foods depend upon context. Thus meat is masculine when opposed to vegetables, but feminine when, as game, it is linked to the hunter. In many parts of Australia, for example, men may refer to women of the 'wife' category as 'right meat,' i.e. legitimate sexual partners.

between a man and his wife's mother. . . . son-in-law and mother-in-law must neither see nor speak to one another; this, at least, prevents the possibility of any competition between a girl and her mother for the affection of the same man—a danger which might be very real where so often the wife is much younger than the husband and the husband and mother-in-law are of the same age; indeed, the former is sometimes older than the latter . . .

In many tribes this avoidance rule is extended to wife's mother's mother, probably because this woman and mother-in-law are in a sense equivalent, inheriting their flesh and blood through the one line of women. . . . apparently the tradition has grown up that it is not wise to have any intercourse with a woman through whom the mother-in-law was incarnated . . .

Further: in many tribes the wife's mother's brother is brought within the range of the same taboo, no doubt because he belongs to the same local clan and country as the mother-in-law . . ., and also because he was incarnated through the womb of the same mother as herself. He is therefore equivalent to her, a male mother-in-law . . .

This avoidance of wife's 'uncle' is not a mere form. He is usually called by a term signifying tabooed, and often it is the term which is used for mother-in-law . . . The avoidance is not so complete as in the case of mother-in-law and son-in-law for the . . . men [in the relationship of wife's maternal uncle and sister's daughter's husband] do see, and may sometimes speak to, one another from a distance. Membership of the one sex group . . . is the explanation of this modification.

Three other classes of men are brought into the range of avoidances between relations by marriage; these are father-in-law, mother-in-law's father and wife's brother. The first two are the husbands of the most tabooed women, and so would have to share the avoidance which primarily concerned their wives . . .
Father-in-law . . . 'found' the wife's pre-existent spirit and later was one of those who arranged that she should be given to her husband. He is therefore in a position of creditor to his son-in-law, while the latter is in a position of 'inferiority' and of indebtedness to his father-in-law. This is expressed in the attitude of reserve and partial avoidance which is adopted between them, and in the making of gifts of food and artifacts to the father-in-law . . .

The mother-in-law's father is in much the same position; he 'found' and provided the mother-in-law and therefore ultimately gave the wife. The natives in many tribes actually express the position in this way . . . Respect is therefore paid to him, gifts made to him, and a rule of restricted social intercourse must be observed . . .

Brothers-in-law usually adopt a somewhat formal attitude towards one another, sitting a little distance apart and talking quietly—certainly not quarrelling. They are, in many tribes, very guarded in the use of each other's names. . . . they are also bound by ties of initiation, an older brother-in-law being the guardian of the younger during the ceremonies; the ritual bond lasts throughout life. One sign of it is the special language (or code of words) which they use in conversation with one another, and which is also an indication of the ceremonial reserve which they must mutually adopt. (Elkin, 1964, pp. 123-7).

The linguist Kenneth Hale (1971) has given us an outstanding semantic analysis of such a 'code of words' in Walbiri. Another kind of 'special language'—actually a distinct vocabulary, with the same sounds and grammatical principles as ordinary language—is used in connection with the mother-in-law and certain other affines. 'In connection with' here should be taken to mean 'in the presence of' or 'in reference to', for, as we have seen, a man may not directly address his wife's mother (Dixon, 1971; Elkin, 1940a, pp. 345-9; Thomson, 1935, pp. 485-6; for a general statement on such specialised languages, see Capell, 1962).

Perhaps the most salient theme in Elkin's summary is that, with the possible exception of the wife's brother, all of the avoided affines derive their 'taboo' status from their relationship to the mother-in-law, who is thus the central affinal figure—in the most profound sense the road to a wife (Farnill, 1963). My Miwuyt informants expressed this by their use of the term *milmarra*: employed in a general way, it could signify any of the relatives Elkin mentions; but specific reference to 'my *milmarra*' invariably denoted the mother-in-law alone.

The mutual avoidance of mother-in-law and son-in-law is striking enough to have engaged the attention of missionaries, adventurers, and casual observers of Aborigines—especially in European-dominated settlements, where traditional proxemic and other norms are challenged.[9] Anthropologists have been, if not more, then at least not less, sensitive. Thus, referring to some of the Kimberley tribes, Phyllis Kaberry (1939, p. 75) notes that

> . . . a girl must avoid all contact with her . . . son-in-law because she feels *kambulo* or shame . . . The feeling of shame and the habit of avoidance were inculcated at an early age, and even children of seven or eight would look discomforted when I pressed them for the name of . . . their [sons-in-law]. The others round about would giggle at their embarrassment and would finally whisper the name to me.

Berndt (1971, pp. 216-17) offers the following as a statement of mother-in-law/son-in-law behaviour in north-east Arnhem Land:

> A . . . [son-in-law] should not act foolishly before . . . [his mother-in-law]; he should be circumspect in her presence and sit at a distance from her . . . There are cases of . . . [mothers-in-law] sharing the same house as their [sons-in-law], but only when a barrier is placed down the middle of the house or room; or, if they sleep outside in the open, another person always sleeps between them.

And from Meggitt (1962, pp. 153-4) on the Walbiri, this:

> Once he is circumcized, the lad cannot approach, speak to, or deliberately look at any ['wife's mother']. He rarely refers to the women in conversation and then only by using their [class] name or the term *gadjin* (shame) . . . Every Walbiri is trained to recognize the foot-prints of each of his fellows, and, whenever a man espies those of his own wife's mother, he carefully erases them with his foot . . .
> The ban on intercourse with mothers-in-law is one of the

[9] Hall (1963, p. 1003) provides the following extensional definition of 'proxemics': '. . . the study of how man unconsciously structures microspace—the distance between men in the conduct of daily transactions, the organization of space in his houses and buildings, and ultimately the layout of his towns.' I consider the term 'unconsciously' here to be unnecessarily restrictive (cf. Edmonson in Hall, 1968, p. 99). For the most recent general statement on proxemics, see Watson (1972).

strongest taboos operating in Walbiri society, and I have never seen any of the accompanying rules broken . . .

The Walbiri continue to avoid mothers-in-law despite countervailing European pressures that often force ['wife's mother'] and ['daughter's husband'] into close contact. If both are riding in a motor-truck, the men stand facing the front and the women sit facing the back. A man who has to enter a building where women are working will not do so without first announcing his identity and then waiting for the ['wife's mother'] to leave.

On government settlements that I visited, the superintendent supervised the distribution of rations but native workers actually handed out the food. . . . consequently each was bound to encounter some ['wife's mother'] in the process. Usually, such women sidled up to the distribution table with heads averted. They held their ration-bags as far from their bodies as possible, so that loose rations could be poured into the bags without any direct physical contact between man and woman. Tinned rations that were handed to other women were thrown to the ground to be picked up by the ['wife's mother']. No words were exchanged.

Accounts such as these are so engaging that one easily forgets that they consist mostly of impressions, intuitions, and non-random observations, with minimal attention to the native categories and standards pertinent to behaviour. That a Kimberley girl is supposed to assume an attitude of 'shame' towards her son-in-law is a solid enough cultural datum: it would seem to be part of a vocabulary of presumed attitudinal states, other parts of which pertain to other culturally-recognized social relationships. Nowhere in the literature on Aboriginal Australia, however, is there anything like such a vocabulary. Further, the existence of a set of terms of this kind can probably be taken to imply a corresponding set of behavioural conventions whereby the relevant attitude may be communicated. If so, what are we to make of such cavalier descriptions as 'not acting foolishly' and 'being circumspect'?—which appear to be several removes from what one has to know in order to act like a proper Aboriginal son-in-law (cf. Goodenough, 1951). And even 'sitting at a distance' implies a native proxemics—perhaps non-verbal but nonetheless pertinent to behavioural propriety (Munn, 1966;

Watson, 1972, p. 14)—about which we are told next to nothing. All of which points to this irony: that despite a century of anthropological research in Aboriginal Australia, despite the gross platitudes of Radcliffe-Brown that are part of virtually every introduction to Aboriginal life, the least rigorous part of our ethnographic record is that which has to do with the etiquette of social affairs.

There is better information on some other aspects of the mother-in-law/son-in-law relationship. Probably the most remarkable of these is the notion that the membership of a man's ritual lodge should exclude not only his wife but her mother as well (Radcliffe-Brown, 1951, pp. 41-2). In most of Aboriginal Australia, it seems to be considered improper, though perhaps tolerable, for the mother-in-law to be a lodge-mate. Much of the data for such a conclusion is covert (Shapiro, 1970b), but there are several direct statements to this effect in the literature (Elkin, 1932b, pp. 304, 308, 1933c, p. 438, 1939, pp. 208, 222; Falkenberg, 1962, pp. 40-1; Piddington, 1970, pp. 340-1; Thomson, 1972, p. 24). It is as if, having defined the wife's mother as an object, Aboriginal thought incorporates her bestowal into its most ready idiom of exchange. A Dieri man should not take the foreskin of a boy of his own matrilineal group; neither, apparently, should he take a woman of his own ritual lodge as a wife or a mother-in-law.[10]

When, however, he finds an appropriate initiate and cuts the meat, is this act sufficient grounds for the victim to lay claim to his daughter as a wife? Much of the literature on Central and Western Australia conveys the impression that men simply give their daughters to the boys they circumcize—which is to say that girls are bestowed directly by their fathers, and that mother-in-law bestowal does not exist. But in what is probably the richest account of affinal rights and obligations in Aboriginal ethnography, Elkin gives the lie to this possibility.

Writing of the desert tribes to the west of the Dieri, Elkin

[10] This analysis is elaborated elsewhere (Shapiro, 1970b), in which I also consider certain alternative explanations of local exogamy regarding the wife's mother. The feasibility of an alliance interpretation is considered below.

(1940a, p. 339) notes that, 'with circumcision . . ., the operator must be in a position to make adequate compensation for what he has done, and as such compensation is everywhere considered to be a wife, he must be a possible wife's father . . . He . . . must . . . give his daughter in marriage to the newly initiated man . . .'. This looks a bit—just a bit—like a marital alliance relationship *á la* Lévi-Strauss, in which males are the agents, females (and 'female' things—see p. 95) the objects.

But matters are not so simple. The wife's mother enters Elkin's picture—though at first only by the back door of her relationship with her husband:

> Marriage contracts and responsibilities are . . . implied in, and arise from, initiation, especially from circumcision. Henceforth the young man enters into *umari* relationships with their duties and avoidances, in particular towards his operator, who is also his wife's father . . . He is also taught who is or are his *umari* women, including one whose daughter is promised to him. She . . . makes fire for him which he then uses . . . during the time of healing . . . Some . . . men told me that it was at this . . . [point] that the young fellow was taught the word *mokuli*, wife's mother, and its significance (p. 341).[11]

Her position improves rapidly. On the very next page there are the following astonishing statements:

> The fundamental [affinal] relationship is that between wife's mother and daughter's husband . . . Such a relationship may be established before either the future husband or wife is born, let alone grown up, or it may be established in later years, especially after the man has reached adulthood and desires to assure himself of a young wife in his old age . . . But as already seen, an important and necessary occasion for arranging betrothal and therefore of establishing the wife's mother-daughter's husband relationship is at circumcision. The mother-in-law gives the youth a firestick, even though she has as yet no daughter. The same ritual establishment

---

[11] The word *umari* is in this area applied to affines, and seems to have the expected 'taboo' connotation. Thus, earlier in the same article, Elkin (p. 333) renders *mokuli umari* as 'father's sister tabooed' and 'wife's mother'. The similarity, in both sound and meaning, to the Miwuyt *mukul rumaru* is striking, especially in view of the fact that speakers of the languages concerned are separated by a thousand miles.

of this relationship bond may take place before the youth is circumcised (p. 342).

Confused? So am I. So, may I suggest, is Elkin. If 'marriage contracts ... arise from ... circumcision', how can they be entered into by older men, by boys not yet circumcized, or by the unborn? And if circumcision is a 'necessary occasion for arranging betrothal', and the circumciser is the wife's father, why is the relationship with the mother-in-law 'fundamental'? *Et cetera.*

On the basis of analogies from other parts of Australia, I would hazard the guess that the following holds with regard to marriage contracts in these desert tribes:

1) Males acquire promises of wives by mother-in-law bestowal, at least sometimes signified by the prestation of the firestick.

2) Females, at the time of their initial bestowal as mothers-in-law, are effectively unmarried and childless. They may, however, be wives and/or mothers at the time of later bestowals (p. 199).

3) Males acquiring mothers-in-law in this way may be of any age, or unborn.

4) Such males, if not yet circumcised, enter into a special relationship at circumcision with the husbands, or husbands-to-be, of their mothers-in-law. This relationship is thus derived from the mother-in-law/son-in-law one, not vice versa.

5) Because of the more marked avoidance enjoined with the wife's mother, males have more conspicuous contact with their fathers-in-law. For this reason anthropologists have been led to believe that these last-named bestow their own daughters.

Do these conclusions apply generally where men are said to give their daughters to boys they circumcise? I believe they do, but I cannot prove it. I do know, though, that mother-in-law bestowal has been remarkably difficult for anthropologists to discover. Hart and Pilling (1960) missed it with the Tiwi. So did Warner (1937) and Berndt (1955, 1965) in north-east Arnhem Land, and, apparently, McConnel (1934, 1940, 1950) and McKnight (1971) with the Wikmunkan, Meggitt (1962) with the

Walbiri, and Hiatt (1965, 1968) with the Gidjingali (cf. Thomson, 1972, pp. 18-19; Peterson, 1969, p. 33, 1970a, pp. 213-14; Hamilton, 1970). Why this should be so is not entirely clear, though I suspect that conclusion (5), just adduced, provides a partial explanation for some of these gaps (see also pp. 114-16). Non-professional observers, at any rate, with (presumably) less ethnographic competence and more of an eye for the bizarre, have noted the institution in at least two cases (Chaseling, 1957, pp. 64-6; Gunn, 1914, p. 33).[12]

But if mothers-in-law are bestowed, who has the right to make the gift? Elkin's summary statements, quoted above, suggest that this right belongs to the mother-in-law's father, a conclusion expressly noted for the Tiwi by Goodale (1962, p. 454, 1971, p. 54). Where this is the case, it is plainly misleading to characterize marital bestowal as a 'matrilineal' affair; for the mother-child link is relevant only in deriving the payoff in the transaction, not the prestation of the initial object. Even so, a Lévi-Straussian interpretation, to the effect that an alliance thus exists between the lodge of the mother-in-law and that of her son-in-law, is unfounded: there is no evidence that the latter individual, and the former's father, enter into the relationship except as private parties.

In north-east Arnhem Land, by contrast, a girl is most properly bestowed as a mother-in-law by her matrikin—usually her mother and maternal uncles, sometimes as far back as her maternal grandmother and *her* brothers. Something like this appears to hold for the Wikmunkan as well (Thomson, 1972, pp. 18-19). In these cases, at least, marital bestowal is less equivocally 'matrilineal'. But what is especially interesting is that my Miwuyt informants also considered it appropriate that a girl's father bestow her as a mother-in-law—though in instances of disagreement, I was told, he is supposed to defer to the wishes of his wife and brothers-in-law. Similarly, McConnel (1940,

---

[12] Spencer and Gillen should really be included here, since neither was a trained ethnographer. I might take this opportunity to acknowledge the assistance of my student Jo Faber, who was kind enough to excerpt for me several of the passages in the literature on mother-in-law bestowal and its associated symbolism.

p. 455) records two instances of what is probably paternal influence in mother-in-law bestowal among the Wikmunkan.

This, then, may well be yet another sphere in which fathers regularly seek to extend their power. If so, it is by no means unlikely that the Tiwi case represents the culmination of these efforts: the stipulation of paternal authority in mother-in-law bestowal, and the complete removal of 'matrilineal' influence from this domain.[13] But this is very close to uninformed speculation; before it can be taken seriously, we need far more hard data on the politics of Aboriginal affinity.

A major step in this direction has been made by Annette Hamilton, in a re-study of Hiatt's Gidjingali. Working with female informants, Hamilton (1970, p. 17) found 'firstly that the ideal model of Gidgingali marriage arrangements as depicted by men'—noted above by Hiatt—'does not constitute an accepted truth for women; secondly that the actual models women use in attributing the power of bestowal are not randomly chosen; and thirdly that the regularities observed in this are a reflection of the age distribution of the parties involved'. Thus, referring to the bestowal of females as wives, Hamilton notes that

> . . . the older a woman is, the more likely she is to nominate a member of the bestowed girl's matrigroup as the bestower; and the younger a woman is, the more likely she is to nominate a member of her own patrigroup [as her bestower]. Young girls believe their fathers bestow them (and have the right to bestow them). Old women believe they have a right to bestow their granddaughters. Shapiro . . . has recently paid considerable attention to . . . [such] 'mother-in-law bestowal'. I have been concerned here merely to document the presence of this model among others in the society, and to indicate where it is used (p. 19).

But Hamilton goes further and attempts to account for this patterning:

> . . . not all the [mother's mothers] . . . claimed to have bestowed their granddaughters themselves; but when the relative ages in these cases are calculated, in each one the father of the child was

---

[13] In a personal communication, Professor Goodale has been kind enough to inform me that such influence seems to be entirely lacking among the Tiwi.

more than seven years older than the child's maternal grandmother [i.e. the father's mother-in-law]. Even where a bestowal was originally made by a mother's mother, the likelihood is high that as the girl, her grandmother and her father all grow older, the relative power of her father comes to greatly exceed that of her grandmother; at 45 a woman becomes a *kapula*, an old one, respected but often ineffective; a man at 45, however, is usually at the peak of his productive capacity . . . So there is both a real difference in bestowal power based on the relative ages and the statuses of the parties involved, and a high likelihood that men in relatively more powerful positions will appropriate a bestowal originally made by a mother's mother (ibid.).

Further, at least in first bestowals, 'there is little likelihood that a mother and mother's brother will be effective', since both are usually adolescent at this time; and 'in Aboriginal society people of this age have no power and are most unlikely to even have an opinion about a suitable future husband for a baby girl, let alone to press their claims over others' (ibid.).

The suggestion, then, is that the neat 'matrilineal' model of bestowal that seems to be fundamental to Aboriginal thought is regularly subverted by three other basic considerations: that Aboriginal men are much older than their wives and brothers-in-law; that age dominates youth; and that men dominate women. All three assertions are subject to qualification; yet all are broadly true.[14] And all, finally, lead us to expect that fathers will often prevail over matrikin not only in giving wives, as Hamilton would have it, but in bestowing mothers-in-law as well (see also Peterson, 1969, p. 33).

Hamilton's remarkable analysis reminds us that marital placement in Aboriginal Australia is a drawn-out process. The eventual prestation of a girl as a wife by her mother and maternal uncles, such as Hiatt reports for the Gidjingali, is probably only a 'moment' in this process—perhaps the fulfilment of an agreement initiated by the bestowal of the mother herself as a mother-in-law (Goodale, 1962, p. 457; Shapiro, 1969a, p. 76).

---

[14] Feminists who object to the last of these assertions need to look at some ethnography. D'Andrade (1967) provides an overview of various pertinent materials.

In north-east Arnhem Land I found that mother-in-law bestowals usually failed to work out as originally intended: hopeful sons-in-law, for example, often died waiting, thus unwittingly commencing new arrangements. And the original bestowers themselves may by this time have departed, leaving the young mother and her brothers to decide the fresh marital placement of the nearly-ripe daughters—perhaps with the unwelcome assistance of their far more senior father. Most accounts of Aboriginal marital politics are probably imprisoned at this point in the process: hence the record of inconsistencies noted by Hiatt and, I suspect, much of the blindness to mother-in-law bestowal.

As for the recipients, most men can thus be expected to get most of their wives—almost certainly their first wives—by procedures other than a girl's first bestowal as a mother-in-law. I therefore doubt that the *tualcha mura* institution is the 'most usual method of obtaining a wife' among the Arunta, as Spencer and Gillen allege. In any case, it is clear that Aboriginal suitors do not put all their ceremonial cords in one basket, that they have other and more direct means of acquiring wives. Equally clear is that, in these efforts, they are more or less subject to certain impersonal constraints, particularly those mentioned in chapters 6 and 7. Even so, as Hiatt (1965, pp. 75-102) and others have shown, they frequently come into conflict with each other, and with bestowers.

Conclusion

I have tried in this book to convey a sense of controversy, of the development and modification of anthropological thought on Aboriginal Australia. Many of you may judge that I have succeeded too well, that I should have paid less attention to the history of anthropology and more to the hard facts. My reply to this is that many of the facts are more than a little mushy; that some have dissolved and vaporized altogether under the heat of debate and ongoing research; and that a few of these have remained, like gaseous ghosts, to haunt the halls of academe.

Unlike many of my colleagues, I believe that it is still possible to dispel these phantoms and to add to our knowledge of traditional Aboriginal cultures through ethnographic research. This is not to understate the degree of change: many Aborigines on Arnhem Land mission stations, for example, live in mission-built cottages, and all those I talked with are aware that young Europeans are supposed to arrange their own marriages. But these and other states of affairs do not—at least not necessarily or yet—point to *cultural* changes, insofar as culture is viewed, as it is here, from a cognitive standpoint. Thus cottage-dwelling Aborigines avow and employ the same principles of co-residence as their less advantaged compatriots (pp. 23-4); and those bold enough to couple European-style still feel compelled to respect traditional categories—and even then their action is judged by others to be 'left-handed' and 'crooked'.

It is now difficult and it will soon be impossible to study Aborigines who still subsist by hunting and foraging: this is a disappointment to ecological anthropologists, to demographers, and no doubt to more romantic students of cultural anthropology. But those of us who take the concept of culture seriously need not be discouraged[1], for we can still proceed more or less as before: we can still talk and listen to people. Indeed, by attending more to what they do with their informants, cultural anthropologists may, as some have argued, be able to get harder facts than ever (Frake, 1964; Metzger and Williams, 1963; Wallace and Atkins, 1965).

[1] For most anthropologists 'culture' is a logically mixed bag which includes both behavioural standards and actual performances and artifacts which result from the application of these standards. Goodenough (1971) and other cognitive anthropologists have taken pains to untangle this mess, and in so doing have brought cultural anthropology remarkably close to certain developments in linguistics and psychology (Greene, 1972; Miller et al, 1960).

References

Aberle, David F. 1961. Matrilineal descent in cross-cultural perspective. In Schneider and Gough (1961).

Adam, Leonhard. 1947. Virilocal and uxorilocal. *American Anthropologist* 49:678.

Adams, Richard N. 1960. An inquiry into the nature of the family. In Dole and Carneiro (1960).

Alland, Alexander. 1963. Residence, domicile, and descent groups among the Abron of the Ivory Coast. *Ethnology* 2:276-81.

Ashley Montagu, M. F. 1937. *Coming into being among the Australian aborigines.* London: Routledge.

——, 1941. Ignorance of physiological maternity in Australia. *Oceania* 12:75-8.

Barnes, John A. 1967. Inquest on the Murngin. *Royal Anthropological Institute Occasional Paper* No. 26.

Basso, Ellen B. 1970. Xingu Carib kinship terminology and marriage. *Southwestern Journal of Anthropology* 26:402-16.

——, 1973. *The Kalapalo Indians of Central Brazil.* New York: Holt, Rinehart & Winston.

Beckett, Jeremy. 1967. Marriage, circumcision, and avoidance among the Maljangaba of north-west New South Wales. *Mankind* 6:456-64.

Berndt, Ronald M. 1955. 'Murngin' (Wulamba) social organization. *American Anthropologist* 57:84-106.

——, 1959. The concept of 'the tribe' in the Western Desert of Australia. *Oceania* 30:81-107.

——, 1962. *An adjustment movement in Arnhem Land.* Paris: Mouton.

——, 1965. Marriage and the family in north-eastern Arnhem Land. In Meyer Nimkoff (ed.). *Comparative family systems.* Boston: Houghton Mifflin.

—— (ed.). 1970a. *Australian Aboriginal anthropology.* Nedlands: University of Western Australia Press.

——, 1970b. Two in one, and more in two. In Jean Pouillon and Pierre Maranda (eds.) *Échanges et communications*. Paris: Mouton.

——, 1971. Social relationships among two Australian Aboriginal societies of Arnhem Land. In Francis Hsu (ed.) *Kinship and culture*. Chicago: Aldine.

——, 1972. The Walmadjeri and Gugadja. In Bicchieri (1972).

——, and Catherine H. Berndt. 1951. Sexual behaviour in western Arnhem Land. *Viking Fund Publications in Anthropology* No. 16.

——, ——, 1964. *The world of the first Australians*. London: Angus & Robertson.

——, ——, (eds.). 1965. *Aboriginal man in Australia*. London: Angus & Robertson.

——, ——, 1970. *Man, land, and myth in North Australia: the Gunwinggu people*. East Lansing: Michigan State University Press.

Bicchieri, Mario G. (ed.). 1972. *Hunters and gatherers today*. New York: Holt, Rinehart & Winston.

Birdsell, Joseph B. 1970. Local group composition among the Australian aborigines. *Current Anthropology* 11:115-42.

Capell, Arthur. 1962. Language and social distinction in Aboriginal Australia. *Mankind* 5:514-22.

Chaseling, Wilbur S. 1957. *Yulengor: nomads of Arnhem Land*. London: Epworth Press.

Chomsky, Noam A. 1965. *Aspects of the theory of syntax*. Cambridge, Mass.: M.I.T. Press.

Crocker, Christopher. 1969a. Men's house associates among the Eastern Bororo. *Southwestern Journal of Anthropology* 25:236-60.

——, 1969b. Reciprocity and hierarchy among the Eastern Bororo. *Man* 4:44-58.

D'Andrade, Roy G. 1967. Sex differences and cultural institutions. In Eleanor Maccoby (ed.). *The development of sex differences*. Stanford: Stanford University Press.

de Leeuwe, J. 1963. The recognized lasting communal living of more than one man with more than one woman. *Bijdragen tot de Taal-, Land- en Volkenkunde* 119:301-16.

Dixon, Robert M. W. 1971. A method of semantic description. In Steinberg and Jakobovits (1971).

Dole, Gertrude E. and Robert L. Carneiro (eds.). 1960. *Essays in the science of culture*. New York: Crowell.

Driver, Harold E. 1966. Geographical-historical *versus* psycho-functional explanations of kin avoidances. *Current Anthropology* 7:131-82.

Dumont, Louis. 1957. Hierarchy and marriage alliance in South Indian kinship. *Royal Anthropological Institute Occasional Paper* No. 12.

——, 1966. Descent or intermarriage: a relational view of Australian section systems. *Southwestern Journal of Anthropology* 22:231-50.

——, 1971. Marriage alliance. In Nelson Graburn (ed.). *Readings in kinship and social structure.* New York: Harper & Row.

Dunning, R. W. 1959. *Social and economic change among the Northern Ojibwa.* Toronto: University of Toronto Press.

Durkheim, Émile. 1915. *The elementary forms of the religious life.* London: Allen & Unwin.

—— and Marcel Mauss. 1963. *Primitive classification.* Chicago: University of Chicago Press.

Edgerton, Robert B. 1964. Pokot intersexuality. *American Anthropologist* 66:1288-99.

Elkin, A. P. 1931a. The kopara. *Oceania* 2:191-8.

——, 1931b. The social organization of South Australian tribes. *Oceania* 2:44-73.

——, 1932a. The secret life of the Australian aborigines. *Oceania* 3:119-38.

——, 1932b. Social organization in the Kimberley Division, North-western Australia. *Oceania* 2:296-333.

——, 1933a. Studies in Australian totemism: sub-section, section, and moiety totemism. *Oceania* 4:65-90.

——, 1933b. Totemism in north-western Australia (part 1). *Oceania* 3:257-96.

——, 1933c. Ibid., part 2A. *Oceania* 3:435-81.

——, 1934. Cult totemism and mythology in northern South Australia. *Oceania* 5:171-92.

——, 1938a. Kinship in South Australia (part 1). *Oceania* 8:419-52.

——, 1938b. Ibid., part 2. *Oceania* 9:41-78.

——, 1939. Ibid., part 3. *Oceania* 10:196-234.

——, 1940a. Ibid., part 4. *Oceania* 10:295-349.

——, 1940b. Sections and kinship in some desert tribes of Australia. *Man* (old series) 40:21-4.

——, 1950. The complexity of social organization in Arnhem Land. *Southwestern Journal of Anthropology* 6:1-20.

——, 1953. Murngin kinship re-examined, and remarks on some generalizations. *American Anthropologist* 55:412-19.

——, 1956. A. R. Radcliffe-Brown, 1880-1955. *Oceania* 26:239-51.

——, 1963. Rethinking anthroplogy: a review. *Oceania* 34: 81-107.

——, 1964. *The Australian aborigines.* Natural History Library edition. New York: Doubleday.

——, Ronald M. Berndt, and Catherine H. Berndt. 1951. Social organisation of Arnhem Land. *Oceania* 21:253-301.

Engels, Frederick. 1942. *The origin of the family, private property, and the state.* New York: International Publishers.

Falkenberg, Johannes. 1962. *Kin and totem.* Oslo: Oslo University Press.

Faris, James C. 1969. Some cultural considerations of duolineal descent organization. *Ethnology* 8:243-54.

Farnill, Douglas. 1963. Aboriginal marriage arrangements. B.A. Honours thesis, University of Sydney.

Fison, Lorimer, and A. W. Howitt. 1880. *Kamilaroi and Kurnai.* Melbourne: George Robertson.

Fox, Robin. 1967a. *Kinship and marriage.* Baltimore: Penguin.

——, 1967b. Review of Meggitt (1962). *Man* 2:329-30.

——, 1969. Alliance and the Australians: a response to Dr. Hiatt. *Mankind* 7:15-18.

——, 1972. Alliance and constraint: sexual selection in the evolution of human kinship systems. In Bernard Campbell (ed.). *Sexual selection and the descent of man.* Chicago: Aldine.

Frake, Charles O. 1964. Notes on queries in ethnography. In A. K. Romney and Roy G. D'Andrade (eds.). *Transcultural studies in cognition.* Menasha: American Anthropological Association.

Freedman, Maurice (ed.). 1967. *Social organization: essays presented to Raymond Firth.* Chicago: Aldine.

Fry, H. K. 1933. Australian marriage rules. *Sociological Review* 25:258-77.

——, 1934. Kinship in Western Central Australia. *Oceania* 4:472-8.

Gale, Fay (ed.). 1970. *Woman's role in Aboriginal society.* Canberra: Australian Institute of Aboriginal Studies.

Gardner, Peter M. 1966. Symmetric respect and memorate knowledge: the structure and ecology of individualistic culture. *Southwestern Journal of Anthropology* 22:389-415.

Goodale, Jane C. 1962. Marriage contracts among the Tiwi. *Ethnology* 1:452-66.

——, 1971. *Tiwi wives.* Seattle: University of Washington Press.

Goodenough, Ward H. 1951. Property, kin, and community on Truk. *Yale University Publications in Anthropology* No. 46.

——, 1956. Residence rules. *Southwestern Journal of Anthropology* 12:22-37.

——, 1965. Rethinking 'status' and 'role': toward a general model of the cultural organization of social relationships. In Michael Banton (ed). *The relevance of models for social anthropology.* London: Tavistock.

——, 1969. Frontiers of cultural anthropology: social organization. *Proceedings of the American Philosophical Society* 113:329-35.

——, 1970. *Description and comparison in cultural anthropology.* Chicago: Aldine.

——, 1971. *Culture, language, and society.* Reading, Mass.: Addison-Wesley.

Goody, Jack. 1961. The classification of double descent systems. *Current Anthropology* 2:3-25.

Gough, Kathleen. 1959. The Nayars and the definition of marriage. *Journal of the Royal Anthropological Institute* 89:23-34.

Gould, Richard A. 1969. *Yiwara: foragers of the Australian Desert.* New York: Scribner.

——, 1973. Australian archaeology in ecological and ethnographic perspective. *Warner Modules* No. 7.

Greenberg, Joseph H. 1968. *Anthropological Linguistics.* New York: Random House.

Greene, Judith. 1972. *Psycholinguistics.* Baltimore, Penguin.

Guemple, D. L. 1971. Kinship and alliance in Belcher Island Eskimo society. In D. L. Guemple (ed.). *Alliance in Eskimo society.* Seattle: American Ethnological Society.

Gunn, Aeneas. 1914. *The little black princess of the never-never.* London: Hodder & Stoughton.

Hale, Kenneth. 1971. A note on a Walbiri tradition of antonymy. In Steinberg and Jakobovits (1971).

Hall, Edward T. 1963. A system for the notation of proxemic behavior. *American Anthropologist* 65:1003-26.

——, 1968. Proxemics. *Current Anthropology* 9:83-108.

Hallowell, A. I. 1955. *Culture and experience.* Philadelphia: University of Pennsylvania Press.

Hamilton, Annette. 1970. The role of women in Aboriginal marriage arrangements. In Gale (1970).

Hammel, Eugene A. 1960. Some models for the analysis of marriage-section systems. *Oceania* 31:14-30.

——, 1966. A factor theory for Arunta kinship terminology. *University of California Anthropological Records* 24:1-19.

Hart, C. W. M. and Arnold R. Pilling. 1960. *The Tiwi of North Australia.* New York: Holt, Rinehart & Winston.

Hempel, Carl G. 1965. *Aspects of scientific explanation and other essays in the philosophy of science*. New York: Free Press.

Hess, Hans. 1970. *The human animal*. New York: Dell.

Hiatt, Lester R. 1962. Local organisation among the Australian aborigines. *Oceania* 32:267-86.

——, 1965. *Kinship and conflict: a study of an Aboriginal community in northern Arnhem Land*. Canberra: Australian National University Press.

——, 1967. Authority and reciprocity in Australian Aboriginal marriage arrangements. *Mankind* 6:468-75.

——, 1968. Gidjingali marriage arrangements. In Lee and DeVore (1968).

——, 1969. Totemism tomorrow. *Mankind* 7:83-93.

—— and Chandra Jayawardena (eds.). 1971. *Anthropology in Oceania: essays presented to Ian Hogbin*. San Francisco: Chandler.

Hocart, A. M. 1937. Kinship systems. *Anthropos* 32:345-51.

Homans, George C. 1961. *Social behaviour: its elementary forms*. New York: Harcourt, Brace & World.

Howitt, A. W. 1891. The Dieri and other kindred tribes of Central Australia. *Journal of the Royal Anthropological Institute* 20:30-104.

——, 1904. *The native tribes of South-east Australia*. London: Macmillan.

Huizinga, Johan. 1955. *Homo ludens: a study of the play element in culture*. Boston: Beacon.

Kaberry, Phyllis M. 1937. Subsections in the East and South Kimberley tribes of north-west Australia. *Oceania* 7:436-58.

——, 1939. *Aboriginal woman*. London: Routledge.

Kaplan, Joanna O. 1972. Cognation, endogamy, and teknonymy: the Piaroa example. *Southwestern Journal of Anthropology* 28:282-97.

Keesing, Roger M. 1966. Kwaio kindreds. *Southwestern Journal of Anthropology* 22:346-53.

——, 1967. Statistical models and decision models of social structure. *Ethnology* 6:1-16.

——, 1969. On quibblings over squabblings of siblings: new perspectives on kin terms and role behavior. *Southwestern Journal of Anthropology* 25:207-27.

——, 1970a. Kwaio fosterage. *American Anthropologist* 72:991-1019.

——, 1970b. Toward a model of role analysis. In Raoul Naroll and Ronald Cohen (eds.). *A handbook of method in cultural anthropology*. New York: Natural History Press.

Kelly, C. T. 1935. Tribes of Cherburg Settlement, Queensland. *Oceania* 5:461-73.

Kernan, Keith T., and Allan D. Coult. 1965. The cross-generation relative age criterion of kinship terminology. *Southwestern Journal of Anthropology* 21:148-54.

Korn, Francis. 1973. *Elementary structures re-considered.* London: Tavistock.

Kroeber, Alfred L. 1952. *The nature of culture.* Chicago: University of Chicago Press.

Lane, Barbara S. 1961. Structural contrasts between symmetric and asymmetric marriage systems: a fallacy. *Southwestern Journal of Anthropology* 17:49-55.

——, 1962. Jural authority and affinal exchange. *Southwestern Journal of Anthropology* 18:184-97.

Lang, Andrew. 1903. *Social origins.* London: Longmans Green.

——, 1905. *The secret of the totem.* London: Longmans Green.

Leach, Edmund R. 1958. Magical hair. *Journal of the Royal Anthropological Institute* 78:147-64.

——, 1961a. Asymmetric marriage rules, status difference, and direct reciprocity. *Southwestern Journal of Anthropology* 17:343-51.

——, 1961b. *Pul Eliya, a village in Ceylon.* Cambridge, England: Cambridge University Press.

——, 1961c. *Rethinking anthropology.* London: Athlone.

——, 1964. Anthropological aspects of language: animal categories and verbal abuse. In Eric Lenneberg (ed.). *New directions in the study of language.* Cambridge, Mass.: M.I.T. Press.

——, 1966. Virgin birth. *Proceedings of the Royal Anthropological Institute* 1966:39-49.

——, 1967. The language of Kachin kinship. In Freedman (1967).

——, 1971. More about 'mama' and 'papa'. In Needham (1971).

Lee, Richard B. 1968. What hunters do for a living, or, how to make out on scarce resources. In Lee and DeVore (1968).

—— and Irven DeVore (eds.). 1968. *Man the hunter.* Chicago: Aldine.

Lévi-Strauss, Claude. 1960. On manipulated sociological models. *Bijdragen tot de Taal-, Land- en Volkenkunde* 116:45-54.

——, 1962. *Totemism.* Boston: Beacon.

——, 1963. *Structural anthropology.* New York: Basic Books.

——, 1966. *The savage mind.* Chicago: University of Chicago Press.

——, 1969a. *The elementary structures of kinship.* London: Eyre & Spottiswoode.

——, 1969b. *The raw and the cooked.* New York: Harper & Row.

Livingstone, Frank B. 1959. A formal analysis of prescriptive marriage systems among the Australian aborigines. *Southwestern Journal of Anthropology* 15:361-72.

Long, Jeremy P. M. 1970a. Change in an Aboriginal community in Central Australia. In Pilling and Waterman (1970).

——, 1970b. Polygyny, acculturation, and contact. In Berndt (1970a).

Lounsbury, Floyd G. 1964. The structural analysis of kinship semantics. In H. G. Hunt (ed.). *Proceedings of the Ninth International Congress of Linguists.* The Hague: Mouton.

Lowie, Robert H. 1920. *Primitive society.* New York: Boni & Liveright.

——, 1928. A note on relationship terminologies. *American Anthropologist* 30:263-7.

Lucich, Peter. 1968. *The development of Omaha kinship terminologies in three Australian Aboriginal tribes of the Kimberley Division, Western Australia.* Canberra: Australian Institute of Aboriginal Studies.

Macknight, Campbell C. 1972. Macassans and aborigines. *Oceania* 42:283-321.

Maddock, Kenneth. 1969a. Alliance and entailment in Australian marriage. *Mankind* 7:19-26.

——, 1969b. Necrophagy and the circulation of mothers: a problem in Mara ritual and social structure. *Mankind* 7:94-103.

——, 1970a. Imagery and social structure at two Dalabon rock art sites. *Anthropological Forum* 2:444-63.

——, 1970b. A structural interpretation of the *mirriri. Oceania* 40:165-76.

Malinowski, Bronislaw. 1913. *The family among the Australian aborigines.* London: University of London Press.

——, 1930. Kinship. *Man* 30:19-29.

Maybury-Lewis, David H. P. 1967. *Akwe-Shavante society.* London: Oxford University Press.

McConnel, Ursula H. 1934. The Wik-Munkan and allied tribes of Cape York Peninsula. *Oceania* 4:310-56.

——, 1940. Social organization of the tribes of Cape York Peninsula, North Queensland. *Oceania* 10:434-55.

——, 1950. Junior marriage systems. *Oceania* 21:107-43.

McKnight, David. 1971. Some problems concerning the Wik-mungkan. In Needham (1971).

——, 1973. Sexual symbolism of food among the Wik-mungkan. *Man* 8:194-209.

Meggitt, Mervyn J. 1962. *Desert people: a study of the Walbiri aborigines of Central Australia.* Sydney: Angus & Robertson.

——, 1964. Indigenous forms of government among the Australian aborigines. *Bijdragen tot de Taal-, Land- en Volkenkunde* 120:163-80.

——, 1965. Marriage among the Walbiri of Central Australia: a statistical examination. In Berndt and Berndt (1965).

——, 1968. 'Marriage classes' and demography in Central Australia. In Lee and DeVore (1968).

——. 1972. Understanding Australian Aboriginal society. In Reining (1972).

Metzger, Duane, and Gerald E. Williams. 1963. A formal ethnographic analysis of Tenejapa Ladino weddings. *American Anthropologist* 65:1076-101.

Miller, George A., Eugene Galanter, and Karl H. Pribram. 1960. *Plans and the structure of behavior.* New York: Holt, Rinehart & Winston.

Miller, Jay. 1972. The priority of the left. *Man* 7:646-7.

Mitchell, William E. 1963. Theoretical problems in the concept of kindred. *American Anthropologist* 65:343-54.

Morgan, Lewis H. 1871. *Systems of consanguinity and affinity of the human family.* Washington: Smithsonian Institution.

——, 1877. *Ancient society.* New York: Henry Holt.

——, 1880. Prefatory note. In Fison and Howitt (1880).

Munn, Nancy D. 1964. Totemic designs and group continuity in Walbiri cosmology. In Reay (1964).

——, 1966. Visual categories. *American Anthropologist* 68:936-50.

——, 1969. The effectiveness of symbols in Murngin rite and myth. In Robert F. Spencer (ed.). *Forms of symbolic action.* Seattle: University of Washington Press.

——, 1973. *Walbiri iconography.* Ithaca: Cornell University Press.

Murdock, George P. 1937. Correlations of matrilineal and patrilineal institutions. In George Murdock (ed.). *Studies in the science of society.* New Haven: Yale University Press.

——, 1949. *Social structure.* New York: Macmillan.

——, 1959a. *Africa: its peoples and their culture history.* New York: McGraw-Hill.

——, 1959b. Evolution in social organization. In Betty Meggers (ed.) *Evolution and anthropology.* Washington: Anthropological Society of Washington.

Murphy, Robert F., and Leonard Kasdan. 1959. The structure of parallel cousin marriage. *American Anthropologist* 61:17-29.

Needham, Rodney. 1962. Genealogy and category in Wikmunkan society. *Ethnology* 1:223-64.

——, 1963. Symmetry and asymmetry in prescriptive alliance. *Bijdragen tot de Taal-, Land- en Volkenkunde* 119:267-83.

——, (ed.). 1971. *Rethinking kinship and marriage.* London: Tavistock.

——, 1973a. Prescription. *Oceania* 43:166-81.

——, 1973b. Introduction. In Rodney Needham (ed.) *Right and left: essays on dual symbolic classification.* Chicago: University of Chicago Press.

Nimuendajú, Curt, and Robert H. Lowie. 1937. The dual organization of the Ramkokamekran (Canella) of Southern Brazil. *American Anthropologist* 39:565-83.

Peterson, Nicolas. 1969. Secular and ritual links: two basic and opposed principles of Australian social organization as illustrated by Walbiri ethnography. *Mankind* 7:27-35.

——, 1970a. Buluwandi: a Central Australian ceremony for the resolution of conflict. In Berndt (1970a).

——, 1970b. The importance of women in determining the composition of residential groups in Aboriginal Australia. In Gale (1970).

——, 1972. Totemism yesterday: sentiment and local organisation among the Australian aborigines. *Man* 7:12-32.

Piddington, Ralph. 1970. Irregular marriages in Australia. *Oceania* 40:329-43.

——, 1971. A note on Karadjeri local organization. *Oceania* 41:239-43.

Pilling, Arnold R., and Richard A. Waterman (eds.). 1970. *Diprotodon to detribalization: studies of change among Australian aborigines.* East Lansing: Michigan State University Press.

Pink, Olive. 1936. The landowners in the northern division of the Aranda tribe, Central Australia. *Oceania* 6:275-305.

Porteus, Stanley D. 1931. *The psychology of a primitive people: a study of the Australian aborigine.* New York: Longmans Green.

Radcliffe-Brown, A. R. 1910. Marriage and descent in North Australia. *Man* (old series) 10:55-9.

——, 1913. Three tribes of Western Australia. *Journal of the Royal Anthropological Institute* 43:143-94.

——, 1918. Notes on the social organization of Australian tribes. *Journal of the Royal Anthropological Institute* 48:222-53.

——, 1931. *The social organization of Australian tribes.* Melbourne: Macmillan.

——, 1951. Murngin social organization. *American Anthropologist* 53:37-55.

——, 1952. The comparative method in social anthropology. *Journal of the Royal Anthropological Institute* 82:15-22.

——, 1956. On Australian local organization. *American Anthropologist* 58:363-7.

Reay, Marie O. 1962. Subsections at Borroloola. *Oceania* 33:90-115.

——, (ed.). 1964. *Aborigines now.* Sydney: Angus & Robertson.

——, 1970. A decision as narrative. In Berndt (1970a).

Reining, Priscilla (ed.). 1972. *Kinship studies in the Morgan Centennial year.* Washington: Anthropological Society of Washington.

Ridington, Robin. 1969. Kin categories versus kin groups. *Ethnology* 8:460-7.

Rivière, Peter G. 1971. Marriage: a reassessment. In Needham (1971).

Róheim, Géza. 1950. *Psychoanalysis and anthropology.* New York: International Universities Press.

Rose, Frederick G. G. 1960. *Classification of kin, age structure, and marriage amongst the Groote Eylandt aborigines.* Berlin: Akademie-Verlag.

——, 1968. Australian marriage, land-owning groups, and initiations. In Lee and DeVore (1968).

Ruhemann, Barbara. 1945. A method for analyzing classifactory relationship systems. *Southwestern Journal of Anthropology* 1:531-76.

Scheffler, Harold W. 1970. Review of Lévi-Strauss (1969a). *American Anthropologist* 72:251-68.

——, 1971a. Dravidian-Iroquois: the Melanesian evidence. In Hiatt and Jayawardena (1971).

——, 1971b. Some aspects of Australian kin classification. *Mankind* 8:25-30.

——, 1972a. Baniata kin classification: the case for extensions. *Southwestern Journal of Anthropology* 28:350-81.

——, 1972b. Kinship semantics. *Annual Review of Anthropology* 1:309-28.

——, 1972c. Afterword. In Thomson (1972).

——, 1973a. Australian kin classification. Paper presented at the International Congress of Anthropological and Ethnological Sciences, Chicago.

——, 1973b. Kinship, descent, and alliance. In John Honigmann (ed.) *Handbook of social and cultural anthropology.* Chicago: Rand McNally.

Schneider, David M. 1961. Introduction: the distinctive features of matrilineal descent groups. In Schneider and Gough (1961).

——, 1972. What is kinship all about? In Reining (1972).

—— and E. K. Gough (eds.). 1961. *Matrilineal kinship*. Berkeley: University of California Press.

Service, Elman R. 1960. Sociocentric relationship terms and the Australian class system. In Dole and Carneiro (1960).

Shapiro, Warren. 1967a. Relational affiliation in 'unilineal' descent systems. *Man* 12:161-3.

——, 1967b. Semi-moiety organization. *Mankind* 6:465-7.

——, 1968. The exchange of sister's daughter's daughters in northeast Arnhem Land. *Southwestern Journal of Anthropology* 14:346-53.

——, 1969a. Miwuyt marriage. PhD thesis, Australian National University.

——, 1969b. Semi-moiety organization and mother-in-law bestowal in northeast Arnhem Land. *Man* 4:629-40.

——, 1969c. Review of Lucich (1968). *Man* 4.

——, 1970a. The ethnography of two-section systems. *Ethnology* 9:380-8.

——, 1970b. Local exogamy and the wife's mother in Aboriginal Australia. In Berndt (1970a).

——, 1971. Patri-groups, patri-categories, and sections in Australian Aboriginal social classification. *Man* 6:590-600.

——, 1973. Residential grouping in northeast Arnhem Land. *Man* 8:365-83.

Sharp, R. L. 1934. Ritual life and economics of the Yir-Yoront tribe of Cape York Peninsula. *Oceania* 5:19-42.

——, 1935. Semi-moieties in north-western Queensland. *Oceania* 6:158-74.

Smith, Philip E. L. 1972. *The consequences of food production.* Reading, Mass.: Addison-Wesley.

Spencer, Baldwin. 1914. *Native tribes of the Northern Territory of Australia.* London: Macmillan.

—— and F. J. Gillen. 1899. *The native tribes of Central Australia.* London: Macmillan.

——, ——, 1904. *The northern tribes of Central Australia.* London: Macmillan.

——, ——, 1927. *The Arunta.* London: Macmillan.

Spiro, Melford E. 1968. Virgin birth, parthenogenesis, and physiological paternity. *Man* 3: 242-61.

Stanner, W. E. H. 1933a. The Daly River tribes, part 1. *Oceania* 3:377-405.

——, 1933b. Ibid., part 2. *Oceania* 4:10-29.

——, 1933c. A note upon a smiliar system among the Nangiomeri. *Oceania* 3:416-17.

——, 1936a. Murinbata kinship and totemism. *Oceania* 7:186-216.

——, 1936b. A note on Djamindjung kinship and totemism. *Oceania* 6:441-51.

——, 1965. Aboriginal territorial organization. *Oceania* 36:1-26.

——, 1967. Reflections on Durkheim and Aboriginal religion. In Freedman (1967).

Steinberg, Danny D., and Leon A. Jakobovits (eds.) 1971. *Semantics.* Cambridge, England: Cambridge University Press.

Strehlow, T. G. H. 1947. *Aranda traditions.* Melbourne: Melbourne University Press.

——, 1965. Culture, social structure, and environment in Aboriginal Central Australia. In Berndt and Berndt (1965).

Tax, Sol. 1937. Some problems of social organization. In Fred Eggan (ed.) *Social anthropology of North American tribes.* Chicago: University of Chicago Press.

Thomas, Northcote W. 1906. *Kinship organisations and group marriage in Australia.* Cambridge, England: Cambridge University Press.

Thomson, Donald F. 1935. The joking relationship and organized obscenity in North Queensland. *American Anthropologist* 37:460-90.

——, 1949. *Economic structure and the ceremonial exchange cycle in Arnhem Land.* Melbourne: Macmillan.

——, 1972. *Kinship and behaviour in North Queensland.* Canberra: Australian Institute of Aboriginal Studies.

Tiger, Lionel, and Robin Fox. 1971. *The imperial animal.* New York: Holt, Rinehart & Winston.

Tindale, Norman B. 1972. The Pitjandjara. In Bicchieri (1972).

Valentine, Charles A. 1963. Men of anger and men of shame: Lakalai ethnopsychology and its implications for sociopsychological theory. *Ethnology* 2:441-77.

von Brandenstein, C. G. 1970. The meaning of section and section names. *Oceania* 41:39-49.

Wallace, Anthony F. C., and John Atkins. 1965. The problem of the psychological validity of componential analyses. In Eugene Hammel (ed.) *Formal semantic analysis.* Menasha: American Anthropological Association.

Warner, W. L. 1930-31. Morphology and functions of the Australian Murngin type of kinship. *American Anthropologist* 32:207-56, 33:172-98.

——, 1933. Kinship morphology of forty-one North Australian tribes. *American Anthropologist* 35:63-86.

——, 1937. *A Black civilization: a social study of an Australian tribe.* New York: Harper.

Watson, O. M. 1972. *Symbolic and expressive uses of space: an introduction to proxemic behavior.* Reading, Mass.: Addison-Wesley.

Webb, T. T. 1933. Tribal organisation in eastern Arnhem Land. *Oceania* 3:406-11.

Wilson, Katrin. 1970. Pindan: a preliminary comment. In Pilling and Waterman (1970).

Worsley, Peter M. 1967. Groote Eylandt totemism and *Le Totémisme aujourd'hui.* In Edmund R. Leach (ed.) *The structural study of myth and totemism.* London: Tavistock.

Yengoyan, Aram A. 1968. Demographic and ecological influences on Aboriginal Australian marriage sections. In Lee and DeVore (1968).

——, 1970. Demographic factors in Pitjandjara social organization. In Berndt (1970a).

Index

Warren Shapiro holds degrees from the City University of New York, The University of Chicago and The Australian National University. He is now Associate Professor and Head of the Department of Anthropology at Livingston College, Rutgers University, New Jersey.

Professor Shapiro spent sixteen months among the Aboriginal peoples of north-east Arnhem Land, studying their social organization. This book is in part the outcome of his research.

Text computer photocomposed in 11 point Sabon
two point leaded and printed on 100 gsm Woodfree Uncoated Offset
at Griffin Press Limited, Netley, South Australia